EVERYTHING YOU NEED TO KNOW WHEN YOU ARE

THIS BOOK

TO BE READ BY ANYONE YOUNGER THAN

THE SECRETS INSIDE THIS BOOK ARE ONLY FOR 10-YEAR-OLDS!

10

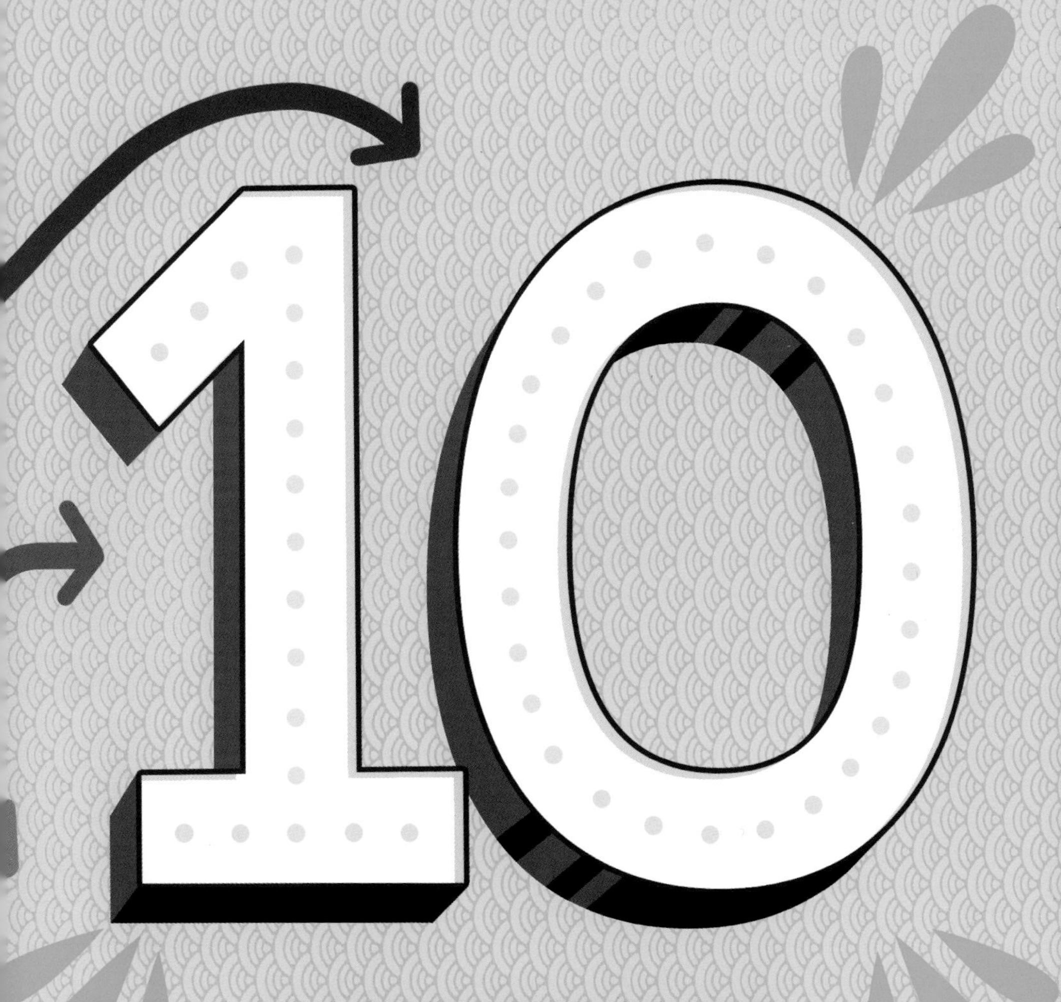

10

NEW YORK TIMES BESTSELLING AUTHOR

KIRSTEN MILLER

ILLUSTRATED BY ELLEN DUDA

AMULET BOOKS • NEW YORK

Cataloging-in-Publication Data has been applied for
and may be obtained from the Library of Congress.

ISBN 978-1-4197-4668-0

Book design by Ellen Duda

Printed and bound in China
10 9 8 7 6 5 4

ABRAMS The Art of Books
195 Broadway, New York, NY 10007
abramsbooks.com

FOR GEORGIA DALY AND CHLOE FLANAGAN

THIS IS A BOOK FOR EVERYONE TURNING

WOOOOOOOOHOOOOOOOOO!

YOU DID IT!

YOU'VE REACHED THE DOUBLE DIGITS!

I bet you've been looking forward to this moment for ages. And you're about to find out that 10 was worth the wait. Ages 8 and 9 were pretty great. **But 10 is the year when things start to get INTERESTING.** *How* interesting, you ask? You may be allowed to set off on adventures WITHOUT ANY ADULTS. You could end up having the WHOLE HOUSE to yourself for hours at a time. People may trust you to watch their small children—and they may even PAY you to play with them. (Ka-ching!) And you know how the stove has been off-limits? Well this year, THAT COULD ALL CHANGE.

That's just the start of it. **It's going to be absolutely amazing.** And this little book is going to help you make sure you squeeze all the goodness out of each and every second of YEAR NUMBER 10.

A FEW THINGS EVERY 10-YEAR-OLD NEEDS

A LIBRARY CARD if you don't have one already!

CRICKETS: FRIED OR BAKED so you can look cool (page 117).

BREATH MINTS to keep your breath fresh no matter what bugs you eat (page 43).

A CALENDAR so you never miss a thing (page 137).

A BLACK LIGHT to reveal secret messages (page 105).

TAPE to tell you if someone's snooping through your stuff (page 25).

A KEY CHAIN since this may be the year you get the keys to your house!

MINI UMBRELLAS for the all the fancy drinks you'll be sipping (page 33).

A GOOD GHOST STORY for breaking the ice (page 49).

FLOWER SEEDS, because you—yes, you—can be a secret superhero (page 149).

"FAST FEET" **AN AWESOME NICKNAME**—why the heck not (page 55)?

SOME VEGETABLE SOUP—you'll find out why...heh heh (page 125).

NINJA SKILLS, of course (page 108)!

WHAT TO DO WHEN SOMEONE HAS A CRUSH ON YOU

You may not know for sure, but you have a hunch there's a person who thinks you're pretty awesome. What are you supposed to do *now*?

FEEL FLATTERED!

It doesn't matter who the kid is. It doesn't matter if you feel the same way! It's nice that someone thinks you're cute, funny, clever, or all-around great, am I right?

BE KIND

Don't feel embarrassed. (Why would you?) Don't run away. And definitely don't be mean. A crush is a compliment. It should make you feel good. So do your best to be nice in return!

IF YOU LIKE THE PERSON, HANG OUT WITH THEM!

You know you like someone when you enjoy spending time together. If that's the case, then the answer is simple: Hang out! Go see movies. Read books together. Challenge them to video games. You're ten years old. You're waaaay too young for boyfriends and girlfriends. But you're the perfect age to have really good friends who you happen to think are super cute and/or charming.

BUT IF YOU AREN'T COMFORTABLE, BE CLEAR

If someone with a crush on you is behaving in a way that makes you upset or uncomfortable, tell them to stop. *Immediately*. Do not hope that they'll just go away. *Make it happen*. If a kid is following you around, ask them to back off. If they're pulling your hair, tell them it's not cool. Say it firmly. Stay calm and be serious. Do NOT get flustered. (When you get upset, they get more attention—which is just what they want.) And if things get too bad, bring in backup. Older brothers and sisters are perfect for this task, but teachers and parents are good choices, too.

A FEW SIGNS SOMEONE GREAT HAS A CRUSH ON YOU

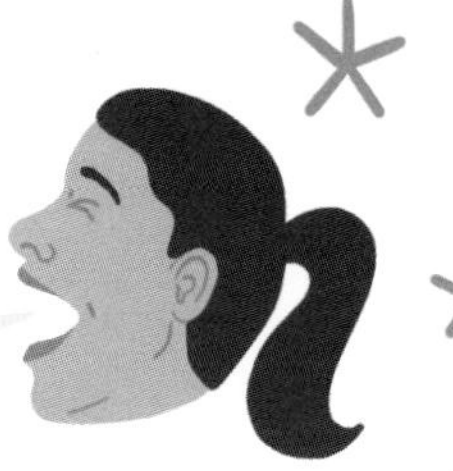

1. THEY LAUGH AT ALL OF YOUR JOKES. EVEN THE REALLY DUMB ONES.

2. THEY DO THEIR BEST TO MAKE YOU LAUGH, TOO.

3. THEY ALWAYS SEEM TO BE NEAR OR NEXT TO YOU.

4. THEY WRITE YOU LOTS OF LITTLE NOTES.

I like you a lot. Let's hang out. xoxo

I THINK U R 2 COOL. —YOUR ADMIRER

5. THEY TRY TO MAKE YOU FEEL GOOD.

6. THEY COME RIGHT OUT AND TELL YOU!

I like you!

I really like you!

WHAT TO DO iF YOU'RE THE ONE WiTH A CRUSH

Someone has caught your eye. Your heart thumps harder when they're near you. Everything they say seems hilarious. OMG! What are you supposed to do? Well go ahead and give yourself a pat on the back. Congratulations, you're human!

You're probably going to have dozens of crushes in your life. (Though if you don't, that's cool, too!) And I'm sorry to report that it never gets any easier. Crushes are confusing—it can be hard to tell when someone likes you back. **Here's the secret to surviving: RELAX.** You're 10 years old. You can have a new crush every week! And if you do it right, having a crush can be super exciting. So just have fun and enjoy it!

TRUST YOUR TASTE

Everybody has their own taste in crushes, and you probably won't like the same boys/girls as your friends. (Which is a good thing, if you think about it!) Different people like different things. You may find you like people who are funny. Or smart. Or daredevils. Or snazzy dressers. Don't expect other people to understand why you like certain traits. That's who you are! Just go with it!

DON'T EXPECT YOUR CRUSH TO LIKE YOU

This is going to sound like bad news, but it's not. Your crush may never like you back. Why? Who knows? Maybe they're not ready for crushes. Maybe they like someone else. If they don't return your crush, don't worry. Just move on to the next cute/smart/funny/daredevil kid.

DON'T BE ANNOYING

Don't follow your crush around like a puppy. Don't play pranks on them. Don't go out of your way to get their attention every minute of the day. Would you like some-one who's acting that way? No. So be cool.

IF THEY TELL YOU TO GO AWAY . . . LISTEN

Sure, it will sting for a little while. But you can't make someone like you. When someone tells you to bug off, that's the end of the story. Move on. The more time you spend feeling bad, the longer it will take to find someone who really *does* want to hang out with you!

THINGS YOU SHOULD NEVER DO TO SOMEONE YOU LIKE:

- ☐ FOLLOW THEM AROUND LIKE A PUPPY.
- ☐ CALL OR TEXT THEM ALL THE TIME.
- ☐ PULL MEAN PRANKS ON THEM.
- ☐ CALL THEM NAMES.
- ☐ IGNORE IT WHEN THEY ASK YOU TO LEAVE THEM ALONE.
- ☐ HUG OR KISS THEM UNLESS THEY GIVE YOU PERMISSION.
- ☐ DO DUMB THINGS TO TRY TO SHOW OFF FOR THEM.

THINGS YOU *SHOULD* DO TO SOMEONE YOU LIKE:

- ☐ BE NICE TO THEM!
- ☐ MAKE THEM LAUGH.
- ☐ BE THERE FOR THEM IF THEY NEED HELP.
- ☐ LISTEN IF THEY'RE FEELING DOWN.
- ☐ TREAT THEM TO ICE CREAM.
- ☐ HANG OUT AND HAVE FUN.
- ☐ SAY A FEW NICE THINGS TO THEM EVERY DAY (BUT DON'T GO OVERBOARD).

HOW TO DO YOUR OWN LAUNDRY

I bet this is something you've been dying to learn! (Kidding!) Laundry may be a chore (though it's better than scrubbing toilets), but it's also a skill that can save you a whole lot of misery.

LEARN HOW TO DO YOUR OWN LAUNDRY AND . . .

1. Your favorite outfit will always be clean when you need it!
2. You'll never get another lecture about rolling around in the mud, sliding through grass, or letting big globs of ice cream drip down your chin!
3. You can wear your brother's/sister's clothes and not get caught when you put them back dirty!

At this point you're probably eager to get started. But you can't just throw clothes in the washer and hope for the best. Follow these rules to do laundry right:

MAKE SURE THE POCKETS ARE EMPTY

One stick of gum or Magic Marker can destroy a whole load of laundry. And don't put anything in the washer that shouldn't get wet. Phones, report cards, and chocolate bars will not survive.

SEPARATE THE LIGHT AND DARK COLORS

The dye in dark-colored clothing may "bleed" in the wash. (Yep, that's the right word.) Do not wash your red socks with your white T-shirts unless you really love pink.

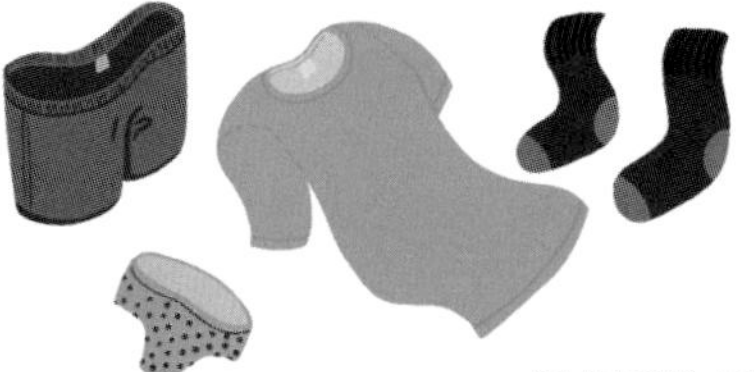

CHECK THE LABELS

Sometimes clothes aren't meant to go in washing machines or clothes dryers. Fancy outfits and sweaters may need to be washed by hand or taken to a dry cleaner. Inside every piece of clothing is a little tag that will tell you exactly how to clean it.

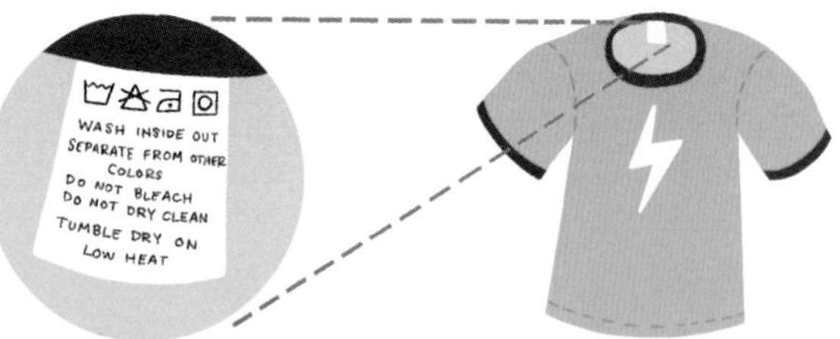

READ THE DETERGENT INSTRUCTIONS

For those of you who've been letting your parents do everything, laundry detergent is *clothes soap*. Not all detergents are the same! Sometimes a little bit goes a long way—and other times you'll need more. The instructions on the back of the box or bottle will tell you just how much to add to the load. (Use too much and you'll be mopping soapy bubbles off the floor.)

ASK SOMEONE TO SHOW YOU HOW TO USE THE MACHINES

It's not hard to use washers and dryers. Anyone can do it. But I don't know what kind of machines you have in your laundry room or laundromat, and there may be a trick or two you need to know. So ask an adult who knows what they're doing.

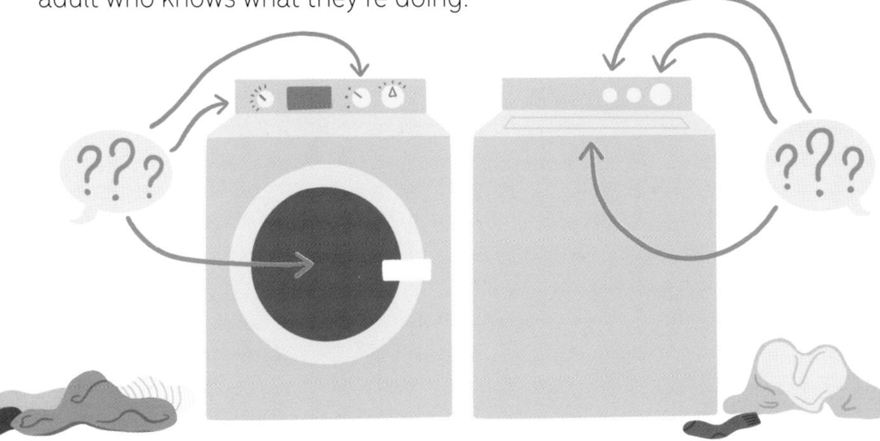

THINGS YOU SHOULD KNOW IF YOU'RE GOING TO BE ALONE IN THE HOUSE

Age 10 is when many kids start spending more time alone in their homes. **CONGRATULATIONS!!!** This means you're growing up. It also means that you need to prove how responsible you can be. If your parents still refuse to let you be alone, showing them that you've mastered the following responsibilities may help convice them that you're mature enough to be trusted.

KNOW WHO YOU'RE ALLOWED TO LET INTO THE HOUSE

What should you do if someone knocks on the door? If it's someone you don't know, it's best not to open the door at all. (Don't worry about being polite.) Even if it's someone you recognize, it might not be a good idea to let them inside. Ask your parents for a list of people who are welcome in your house when you're home alone. The list will probably be much, much shorter than you think.

KNOW WHO TO CALL IF SOMETHING GOES *KINDA* WRONG

Make sure there's a phone handy. Dial 911 for real emergencies. But you should also know who to call if your little brother gets his head stuck between the stair railings—or a bat flies down the chimney. Make sure the phone numbers are programmed into the phone or posted on your fridge.

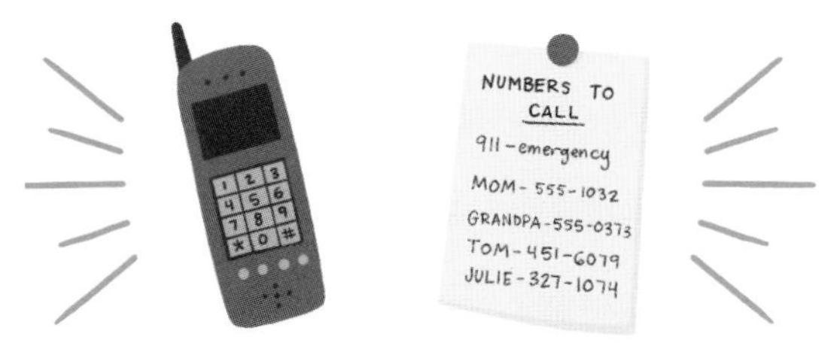

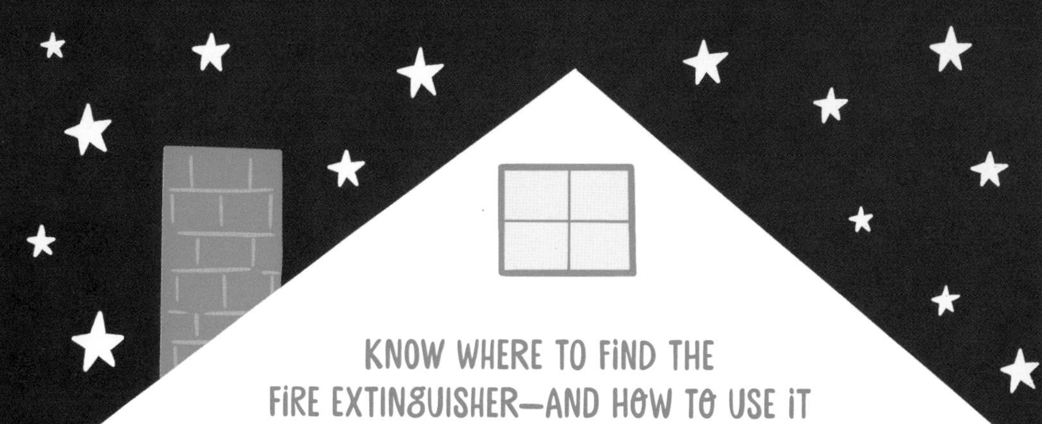

KNOW WHERE TO FIND THE FIRE EXTINGUISHER—AND HOW TO USE IT

If your house doesn't have one, ask your parents to get one. Read the instructions and learn how to use it! (But don't use it unless it's absolutely necessary. You can't even imagine the mess a fire extinguisher will make.)

KNOW WHAT TO DO IF THE TOILET OVERFLOWS

Somewhere on the wall behind your toilet is a knob. Go look for it right now. See it? That knob is super important. If your toilet is overflowing (or looks like it might), turn that knob all the way to the RIGHT. This will turn the water off and prevent the toilet from destroying your whole house.

KNOW HOW TO AVOID STARVATION

You should have learned all about this at age 9. Let's just say the sandwich is your savior, my friend. (Or see this book's chapter on eating bugs!)

KNOW WHAT TO DO IF YOU OR SOMEONE ELSE BEGINS TO CHOKE

If you don't know the Heimlich maneuver, go back and read *Everything You Need to Know When You Are 9*. Or in a pinch, follow the instructions below:

1. Make the person stand up.
2. Bend them forward a bit and use the heel of your hand to give them five hard whacks on the back. This might be enough to knock the food out.
3. If not, get behind the person and wrap your arms around their waist.
4. Make a fist with one hand. Put it right above their belly button with your thumb sticking into their stomach.
5. Grab the fist with your other hand.
6. With a quick, powerful movement, pull your fists backward and upward, into their stomach.
7. Make the same movement five times in a row.

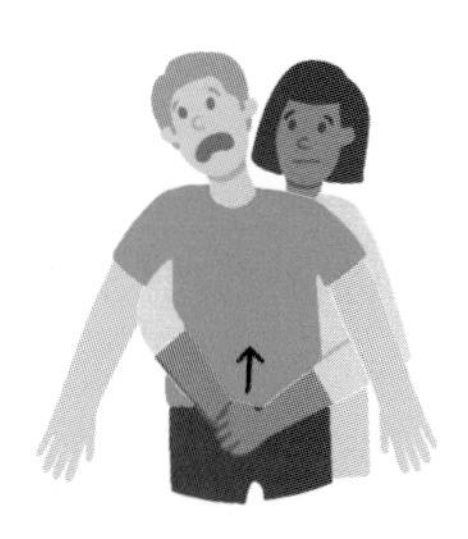

WHAT TO DO IF YOU NEED YOUR PRIVACY

One of the biggest problems many 10-year-olds face is people bugging them! Parents barge into your room with no warning. Sisters and brothers won't give you any peace. You're in the double digits now! You deserve to be left alone!

Everyone needs some time by themselves. Even the friendliest people can get cranky if they aren't allowed to relax. (Just ask my little brother and sister how cranky I used to get!) Now that you're 10, you may start to find that you crave your privacy. If so, here's what to do:

TELL YOUR FAMILY WHAT YOU NEED

So here's a really good piece of advice: **If you want something, ask for it!** You'd be surprised how many people skip this step—then act completely surprised when they don't get their way. If you need an hour or two by yourself, ask everyone in the house to give you your space! More often than not, they'll let you have it. If not, just pick from the next options.

GO TO YOUR SECRET LAIR

Every 10-year-old should have a secret hiding place. (For those who haven't found one yet, be sure to read the next chapter!) This is the place in or near your house that is yours and yours only. Make sure it is well stocked with reading material, snacks, potpourri, a disco ball, and anything else you need to relax.

HEAD FOR THE LIBRARY

When I was a kid, I loved the library. The books were great, but the best part was being left alone. I'd find a deserted aisle (usually the one with the books about ghosts and aliens), sit on the floor, and spend some quality time reading about all of my favorite things.

TAKE A LONG BATH

You know why people take long baths? Yeah, sure, they'll get you clean, but more importantly, they help you escape from everyone else in the house. (Why do you think your mom likes them?) Now that you're 10, I think you can make a pretty good case for locking the door when you bathe. Then throw some bubble bath in the water, lay back, and enjoy some sibling-free time!

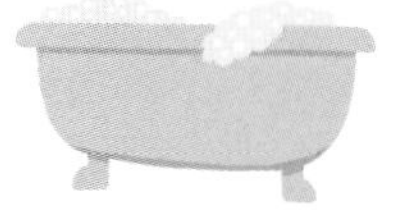

NEED A SECRET LAIR?

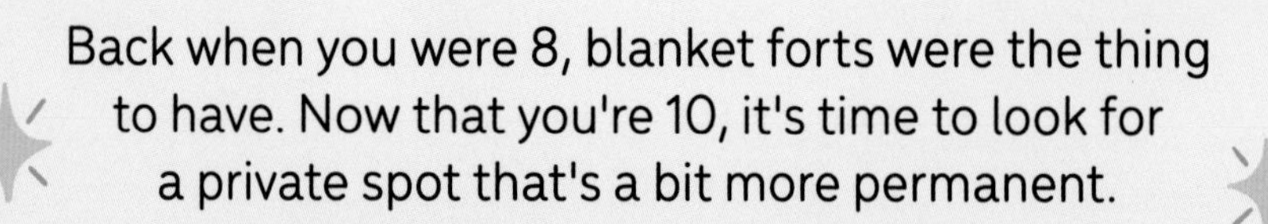

Back when you were 8, blanket forts were the thing to have. Now that you're 10, it's time to look for a private spot that's a bit more permanent.

Bedrooms are no good—everyone knows to look for you there. **It's not a secret lair unless it's a SECRET!**

If you live in a castle or a creepy old mansion, it shouldn't be very hard to find a place to hide when you need to get away from it all. (And by "it all" I mean your relatives.) But for those of you who live in apartments (like me) or ordinary-size houses without lots of nooks and crannies, no worries! If you're searching for a secret lair, just find the perfect closet. (Empty cabinets can work nicely, too. But closets tend to be more spacious.)

THE PERFECT CLOSET CHECKLIST:

- ☐ Isn't used by your family every day.
- ☐ Has enough room at the bottom for the things you need.
- ☐ Isn't filled with spiders and doesn't smell like stinky sneakers.
- ☐ Has a rack of clothing or coats you can hide behind.
- ☐ Contains a secret passage to a magical world.

ONCE YOU'VE FOUND YOUR LAIR, HERE'S HOW TO DECORATE IT:

- ☐ A light you can stick on the wall.
- ☐ A few cushions. A fake sheepskin rug from IKEA would be lovely.
- ☐ Entertainment. (This would be an excellent place to read *The Chronicles of Narnia*.)
- ☐ A houseplant. (Find a nice fake plant—real plants don't love secret lairs.)

HOW TO TELL IF SOMEONE'S BEEN SNOOPING THROUGH YOUR STUFF

Now that you're 10, your privacy is important. Even if you don't have any secrets, you probably don't want people going through your things.

It can be hard to keep people from snooping—especially if you have brothers and sisters. Maybe you suspect someone's been sneaking into your room or going through your dresser drawers, but you want to be sure before you complain. If that's the case, here's how to gather the proof you need:

CLEAR TAPE

Tape can tell you whether a drawer or a door has been opened. Take a small strip of tape and place it over the crack. Try to put it somewhere it won't be seen. If the tape is broken the next time you check, you'll know you've had an intruder.

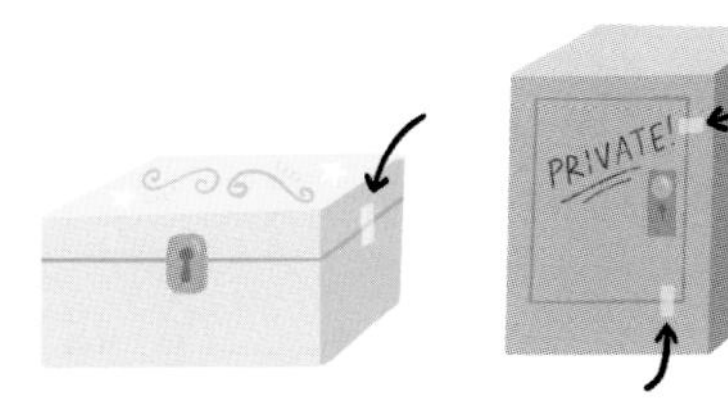

A HAIR OR PIECE OF THREAD

Want to know if someone has opened your private journal? Take a stray hair or a piece of thread and place it in between 2 pages. If it's gone the next time you thumb through the journal, someone may have been reading your juiciest secrets.

PICTURES

Before you leave your room, take a few pictures. When you come back, check the pictures to see if anything was moved while you were gone.

ALARMS

This may be a stretch, unless you're super serious and you've found a way to make some bucks. But if you're at your wits' end, you can find simple alarm systems at any hardware store. They're loud enough to scare the heck out of anyone who opens your bedroom door—and you won't even need tools to set them up!

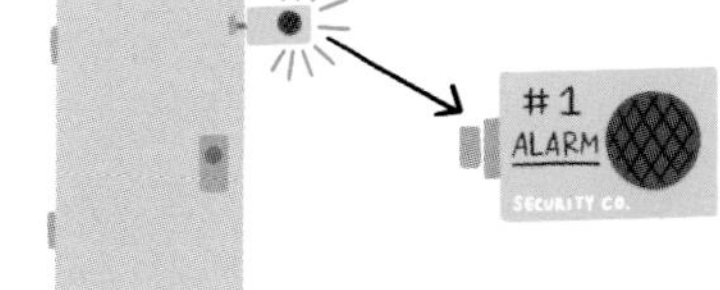

I am not your mom. (Surprise!) I'm not your dad, either. (Duh.) So I can't decide when you're ready to start using the stove. You need to have your parents' permission. (Yes, this is essential.) If they're not sure you're ready, I suggest going back to *Everything You Need to Know When You Are 8*, rereading the chapter "How to Convince Adults That You're Super Mature," and trying again later.

You got permission? Congratulations! This is a big step forward! To celebrate this glorious occasion, I'm going to teach you how to make beef Wellington. Just kidding! We're going to start off with something that (almost) everyone loves. RICE KRISPIES TREATS! They're easy, delicious, and perfect for bake sales (if you're looking to make some big bucks for a personal alarm system). **You need:**

* **A PAN THAT IS ABOUT 9 INCHES WIDE AND 11 INCHES LONG**

* **5 TABLESPOONS OF BUTTER** (Look at the stick of butter. See those little lines along the side? Each of those is a tablespoon. Count five lines and cut the stick of butter there. That's five tablespoons!)

* **6 CUPS OF MINI MARSHMALLOWS** This isn't health food, folks.

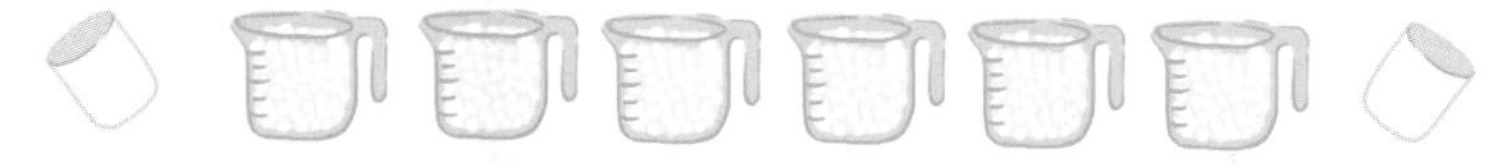

* **6 CUPS OF RICE KRISPIES** Or another similar cereal.

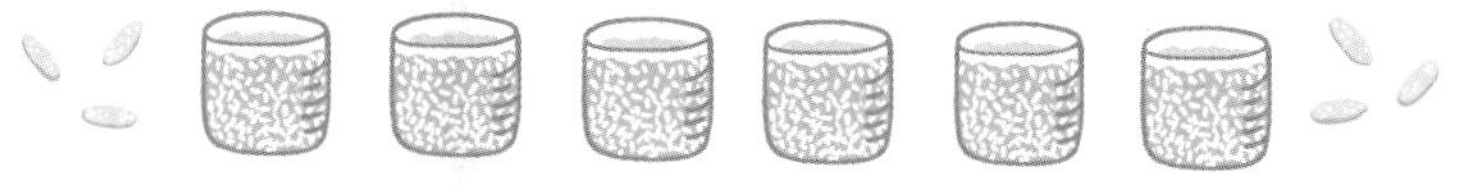

* **EXTRAS** Extras are things you can mix in to make your Rice Krispies treats more colorful or unusual. They're fun, but they're not necessary. I personally prefer my Rice Krispie treats plain, but if you want to give yours a little pizazz, you can add:
    * Food coloring
    * Sprinkles
    * Chocolate chips
    * Freeze-dried fruit
    * Smashed Oreos
    * Nuts (just make sure no one's allergic)

GOT EVERYTHING YOU NEED? OKAY, LET'S GET STARTED!

1. Put the butter in a big pot. Put the pot on the stove and turn the burner on MEDIUM. Melt the butter.

2. When the butter has melted, stir in the mini marshmallows, one cup at a time. Keep stirring until the marshmallows have melted.

3. Turn off the burner. (Be careful! It will still be hot.) Add your extras and stir in the Rice Krispies until everything is mixed up.

4. Spoon the mixture into the pan. Let it cool down just a little. Then press the mixture down with your fingers until the Rice Krispie Treats are flat on top.

5. Let it cool down even more before you cut it!

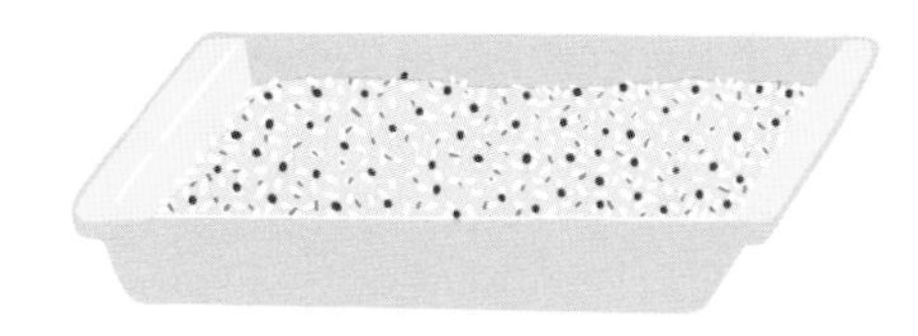

6. EAT!

OR . . . MAKE RICE KRISPIE MONSTERS!

Wait until the Rice Krispie mix has cooled down in the pot enough to touch. Then rub your hands with butter (so the mix won't stick) and mold the mix into any shape you like! Use your "extras" to give your creations eyes, teeth, nostrils, and hair. If you don't like monsters, you can always make snow people. (Yawn.)

As you know by now, I'm a big fan of trying new things. How do you know if something's gross unless you taste it? Maybe you've been missing out on something wonderful your whole life! For example, outside of America, many people would say mixing peanut butter and jelly is disgusting. AND THEY COULDN'T BE MORE WRONG!

HERE ARE A FEW COMBOS FOR YOU TO TRY!

1. PEANUT BUTTER & PICKLE SANDWICHES:
Pickles taste great on everything.

2. CREAM CHEESE & CUCUMBER SANDWICHES:
Try cream cheese with olives or bacon, too.

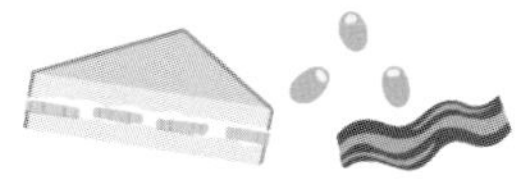

3. HAM & CANTALOUPE:
Sound gross? Very fancy people all over the world love this combo.

4. HONEY & SCRAMBLED EGGS:
This was the only way I would eat eggs when I was a kid.

5. CHEESE & JAM:
They're great together on a sandwich or without any bread.

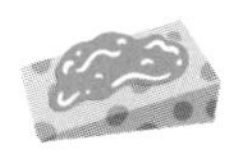

6. FRIES & MAYONNAISE:
I've also heard bananas and mayonnaise make a great sandwich. I'll let you try it first.

7. CHOCOLATE CHIP COOKIES & CHEESE:
Two awesome things that taste awesome together.

8. POTATO CHIPS & CHOCOLATE SYRUP:
Ditto about the sandwich.

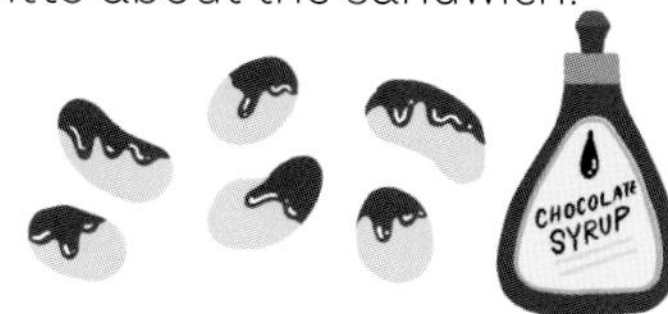

9. SALAMI & GRAPES:
Wrap two grapes in a piece of salami and give your "salami surprise" to a friend to try.

10. ORANGE JUICE & CEREAL:
Not for me, but some people looooove it.

HOW TO
INVENT
YOUR OWN
FANCY
DRINKS

I'm going to put my foot down about this one. Now that you've turned 10, *you deserve fancy drinks with paper umbrellas and cool garnishes*. Seriously—why should adults get to have all the fun? Fortunately, it's easy to make your own fancy drinks! Here's what to do:

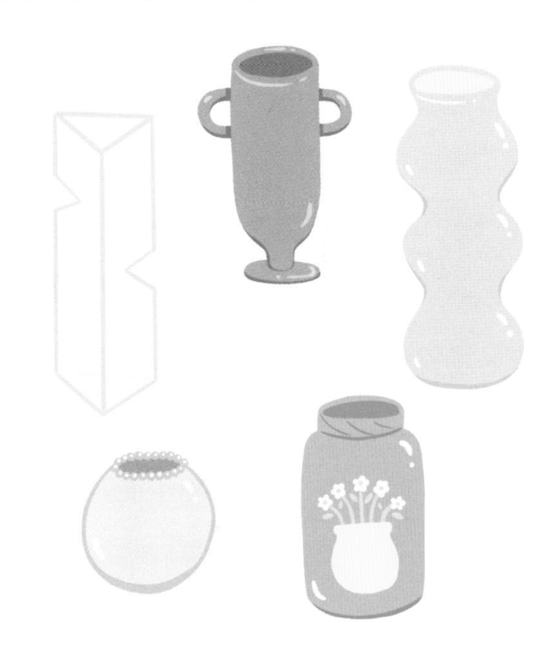

1. FIND AN AWESOME CONTAINER.

Be as creative as you like! Any clean, clear container that can hold liquids and is safe to drink from will work! So find your prettiest glass, coolest jar, or weirdest vase.

2. FILL IT HALFWAY WITH YOUR FAVORITE LIQUIDS

I'm not a huge fan of sodas—especially when it comes to making drinks like this. Juices look sooo much better and they're easy to mix so you get just the right color.

3. ADD A TEENSY BIT OF SYRUP

No, not pancake syrup! Try a fruit syrup like grenadine (which is made from pomegranate juice). If you don't have any, that's totally fine. There are a million other ways to make your drink pretty.

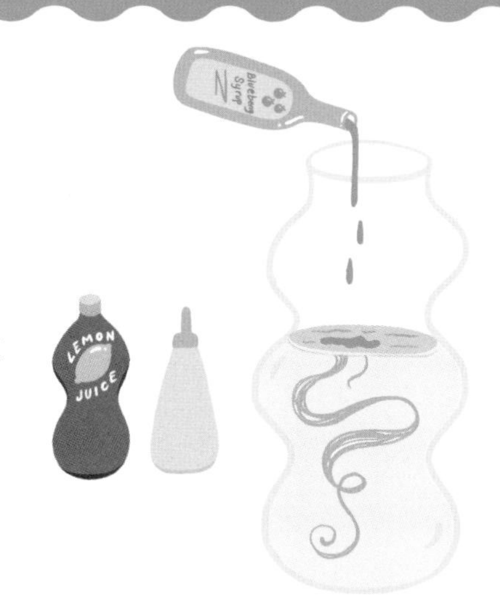

4. CHOOSE FIZZY . . .

If you like your drinks fizzy, just add seltzer! My motto is: Everything in life (baths, gum, fancy drinks) is better with bubbles!

5. . . . OR FROZEN

You'll need a blender—and an adult's permission. (I'm serious. Blenders are super dangerous if not used correctly.) Got permission? Okay. Pour your fancy drink in. Add a few ice cubes. Make sure the top is on before you press any buttons! Is it on? Great. Blend away!

6. THROW IN SOME FRUIT (OR VEGETABLES)

This is when you start getting super creative. A lot of fancy drinks come with slices of lemons or oranges. Cherries and olives are good choices, too. Berries always look amazing. But to be honest, you can plop just about any fruit or vegetable into your fancy drinks. I personally like cucumber and radish slices.

7. CHOOSE A GARNISH

Garnishes are things you use to decorate your drinks. Mini umbrellas are my favorites. Cool-looking straws are great, too. But use your imagination! Anything that's safe to put in a drink (ask an adult) can be used as a garnish. Gummy worms? Heck yeah! Lollipops? Absolutely!

8. MAKE STUNNING ICE CUBES

You'll have to plan ahead for this one. Fill an ice cube tray with water, then add clover flowers or mint leaves. When the water freezes, they'll be trapped in the ice! Or you can fill your ice cube trays with dark juice. If you put your ice cubes in light-colored juice (lemonade is perfect), they'll look like gemstones.

WHAT DOES IT MEAN IF YOUR PEE ISN'T YELLOW

When you were 9, we discussed whether or not it's okay to look at your poop. (Reminder: It's totally cool.) This year, let's talk about pee (which doctors prefer to call *urine* for some reason).

It may surprise you to learn that urine can come in a whole rainbow of colors. (Yes, even blue.) Unfortunately, your pee should really only be one boring color—yellow. As with poop, if your pee is a color it's not supposed to be, the first thing you should do is try to remember what you've swallowed in the past day. That may help explain why your pee is so pretty. If not, you'll want to have it checked out.

CRYSTAL CLEAR PEE

Your pee should be at least a teensy bit yellow. If it's completely clear, you may have been chugging too much water. What's the rush? Slow down!

VERY DARK YELLOW PEE

You need more water. Go grab a glass or two right away.

PINK PEE

Did you recently eat beets, rhubarb, or blueberries? Dark red or purple fruits and vegetables can make your pee turn pink temporarily. If your pee is still pink the next time you go to the bathroom, tell your parents. If it's red, don't wait. Let someone know right away.

GREEN OR BLUE PEE

Whoa! That's gotta be weird looking! Did you eat anything with a lot of blue or green food coloring? Are you taking medicine that can make your pee turn colors? (Have a look at the information that came with it.) That could be the answer. If not, go grab your mom or dad and let them have a look.

ORANGE OR BROWN PEE

Drink some water right away. You could be dehydrated. If your urine doesn't return to light- to medium-yellow soon, have it checked out by a doctor. (They find pee just as fascinating as I do!)

WHAT TO DO WHEN YOUR BODY iS CHANGiNG

DON'T TURN THE PAGE.
I promise—this isn't going to embarrass either of us!

So you've probably noticed that your body is *always* changing. **That's a good thing!** Just think about it: 10 years ago, you were too little to even wipe your own butt! Now you're big enough to do it without much help at all. (That's a joke.)

Around 10, you start to go through some of the biggest changes of your entire life. (Don't worry, I said *start*. Nothing's going to happen all at once.) For instance, I'd bet your feet are a lot bigger than they were last year. Well, soon the rest of you will be growing up, too.

MAYBE THIS MAKES YOU FEEL WEIRD. IT SHOULDN'T. WANT TO KNOW WHY?

Because, if you're a boy,
HALF THE PEOPLE ON THE ENTIRE PLANET HAVE GONE THROUGH THE SAME EXACT THING.

And if you happen to be a girl,
THE *OTHER* HALF HAVE GONE THROUGH THE EXACT SAME THING.

THIS IS IMPORTANT. HERE'S WHAT IT MEANS:

Who's your favorite celebrity?
Yep, they went through it.

Who's the greatest sports star on earth?
That's right. They did, too.

That mean old lady with the feisty chihuahua?
Believe it or not, she was your age once.

Every single kid in your class?
They're going through it right now.

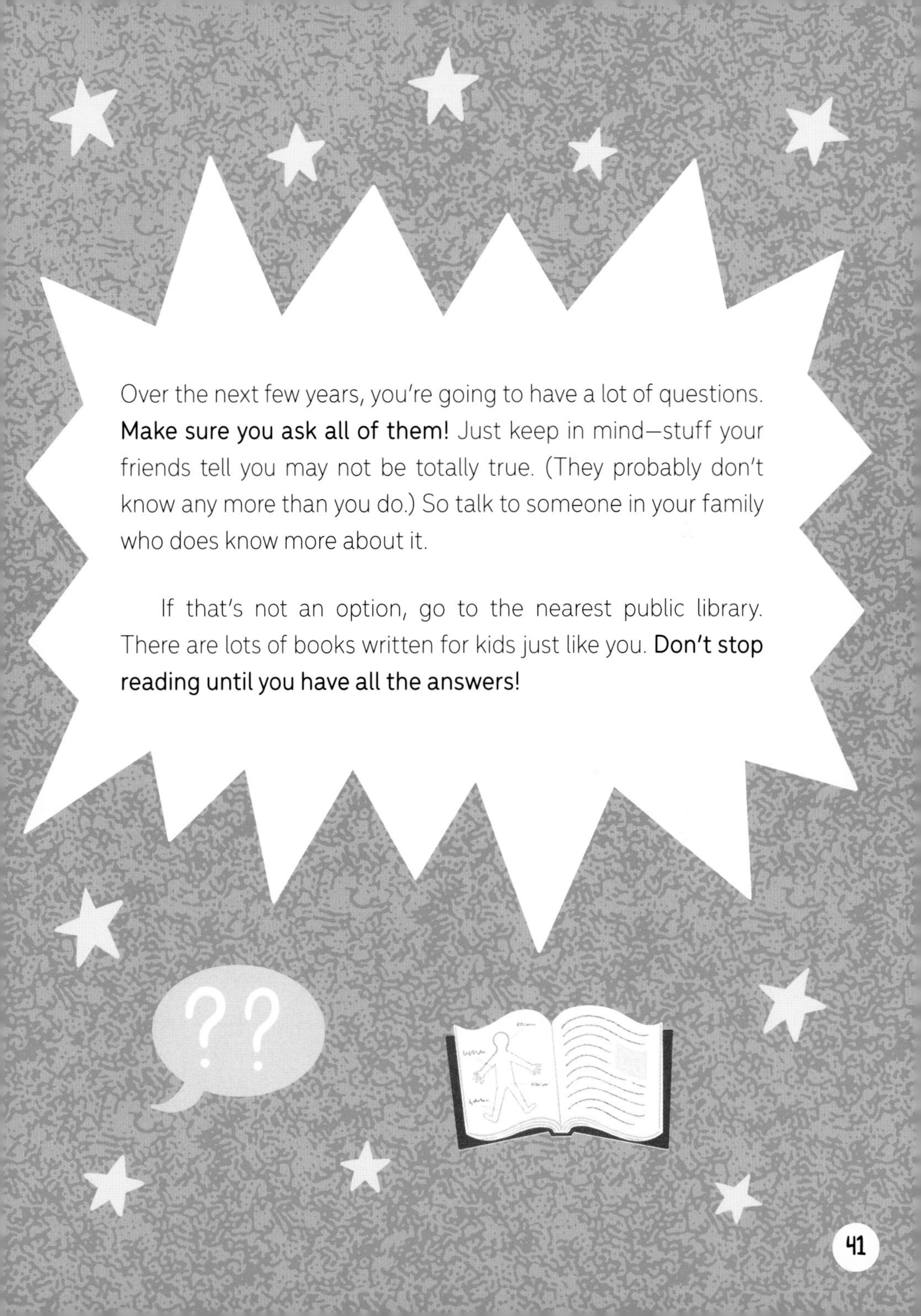

Over the next few years, you're going to have a lot of questions. **Make sure you ask all of them!** Just keep in mind—stuff your friends tell you may not be totally true. (They probably don't know any more than you do.) So talk to someone in your family who does know more about it.

If that's not an option, go to the nearest public library. There are lots of books written for kids just like you. **Don't stop reading until you have all the answers!**

WHAT TO DO iF YOU ARE STiNKY

When you were 8, we discussed how to smell fantastic. Mostly it invovled taking baths. (They really work.) Now that you're 10, you should be taking a shower or a bath much more often. And you may even find that certain parts need a little extra help smelling great. If so, here's what to do!

FEET

They need to be washed every day! Make sure you get between the toes. If your skin looks flaky, red, or raw, you may need to get some athlete's-foot cream.

CLOTHES

Again, washing things magically makes them smell better. Now that you're 10, you don't have to wait for someone to wash your stuff for you. Just read page 12 and do your own laundry!

BUTT

Wash it every day. If it needs a little extra cleaning between showers, just use a wet wipe or a damp piece of toilet paper.

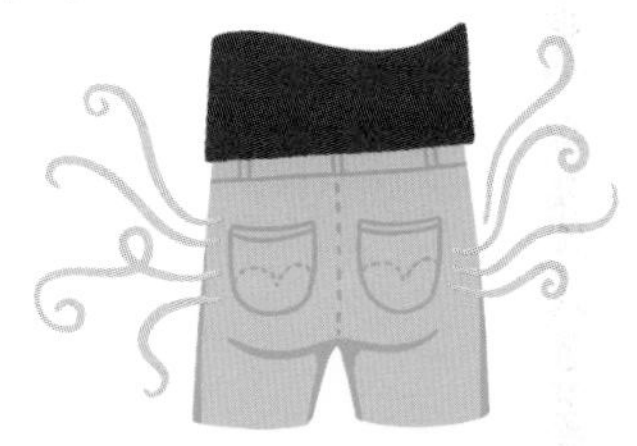

SHOES

Always wear socks when you can, and don't wear plastic shoes. If your sneakers reek, try taking out the insoles and washing them.

UNDERARMS

At some point soon, your underarms are going to start to get a bit stinky. DO NOT FREAK OUT. It happens to everyone, and it's super easy to fix. Just grab some deodorant. It's really that simple. Start by using one for sensitive skin.

BREATH

Brush your teeth twice a day. You know what, go ahead and brush your tongue, too. Don't eat any raw onions unless you have breath mints on hand and you should be good to go!

WHAT TO DO IF YOU WISH YOU LOOKED DIFFERENT

The first thing you should know is that almost everyone in the world feels this way at some point. It's just one of the many weird things about humans—we're never satisfied.

I'm not going to tell you that it's wrong to wish you looked different. How can it be? **Everyone does it!** But don't waste your time worrying about little stuff. You want to sit around wishing your hair was brown or your nose was smaller? Knock yourself out. But there are way better things you could be doing. Here's my advice:

IF YOU CAN'T CHANGE IT, *OWN* IT

Is there something you don't like that you have the power to change (like a hideous haircut)? Then by all means go for it. But if you can't change something (like that gap between your teeth), you might as well *own it*. What does that mean? It means instead of trying to hide it, flaunt it. **Instead of feeling embarrassed, be proud.** Nothing is more attractive than confidence. (See the next chapter for more on this subject!)

DON'T LOOK LIKE EVERYONE ELSE? GOOD!

A lot of people always do their best to blend in. They wear what everyone else wears. They style their hair the same way. They wish they could look even more like their friends. These people grow up to be boring. It's the kids who don't try to be anyone other than themselves who go on to great things. **If you're going to take over the world, you can't be afraid to stand out.**

THINGS YOU DON'T LIKE NOW MAY BE THINGS YOU LOVE LATER

You're just going to have to trust me on this one. **Someday, you may discover that the mole on your face is really a *beauty mark*.** Or your nose isn't big, its *distinguished*. Or your crazy hair can transform into *gorgeous* curls. These transformations happen all the time. (And if you're still unhappy when you get older, you can buy an amazing wig!)

THE MOST IMPORTANT THiNG* YOU CAN BE

If you want the next 70 or 80 years to be awesome, there's one thing you need to be. Some people will say "GOOD LOOKING!" Those people are *wrong*. Other people will say "RICH!" or "BRILLIANT!" Those people are *wrong*, too.

If you want to lead your best life, the most important thing you can be is **SELF-CONFIDENT.** (Along with INTERESTING, which we covered in *Everything You Need to Know When You Are 9*, and KIND.) I like to think of confidence as being comfortable with who you are—and believing that you can do *anything*.

People with confidence walk tall—they don't slump. They look others right in the eye. They speak calmly and clearly. They stand up for themselves when they need to. And they never feel the need to put others down.

Okay, but why is it so important?

IF YOU BELIEVE YOU CAN DO ANYTHING, YOU JUST MIGHT SUCCEED

There are going to be people in your life who will happily tell you all the things you *can't* do. **But if you believe in yourself, you'll be willing to work harder.** You'll keep trying and you won't give up, no matter what. And the more you try, the more likely you are to succeed!

CONFIDENCE SCARES BAD GUYS AND BULLIES

Want to keep bullies and bad guys away? Look like someone who's going to stand up for themselves! (Even if you're secretly scared as heck). Bullies are big cowards. A lot of them aren't looking for a *fight*—they're just looking for someone who will be easy to pick on. Don't let them think for one second that you'll be the type.

OTHER PEOPLE LIKE TO BE AROUND CONFIDENT PEOPLE

Look at the people who have the most friends. (Maybe you're one of them.) What do they all have in common? Maybe some of them are cute. Some may be smart. But I bet you a gazillion dollars all of them are confident. **Because they believe in themselves, other people believe in them, too!**

10
GREAT
CONVERSATION
STARTERS

Even if you're super confident, it's often hard to get a conversation started when you meet someone new. You can ask all the regular questions . . . *Where do you live? What school do you go to? What grade are you in?* Blah, blah, blah. But is that really what you want to talk about? No. So why not skip all the dull stuff and chat about something interesting!

Here's how to do it.

HI THERE, I'M (INSERT YOUR NAME) . . .

1. HAVE YOU EVER SEEN A GHOST?
2. WHAT'S YOUR FAVORITE KIND OF SLIME?
3. WHAT FAMOUS PERSON DO YOU THINK MIGHT BE AN EXTRATERRESTRIAL?
4. HAVE YOU EVER INVESTIGATED OR SOLVED A CRIME?
5. WHAT'S THE WEIRDEST THING YOU'VE EVER SEEN?
6. IF YOU COULD CHOOSE ANY ANIMAL ON EARTH FOR A PET, WHAT WOULD IT BE?
7. WHAT MONSTER WOULD YOU LOVE TO SEE IN PERSON?
8. IF YOU COULD HAVE ONE SUPERPOWER, WHAT WOULD YOU CHOOSE?
9. IF SOMEONE TOLD YOU THERE WAS BURIED TREASURE IN YOUR NEIGHBORHOOD, WHERE DO YOU THINK IT WOULD BE?

Yes, there are going to be people who think you're weird for asking. These people are boring. Find someone else to talk to!

SHOULD YOU EVER CARE WHAT OTHER PEOPLE THINK OF YOU?

At some point soon, an adult will probably tell you that you shouldn't care what other people think. (Maybe you've heard this already!) This is usually very good advice.

YOU SHOULDN'T CARE IF PEOPLE THINK YOU'RE WEIRD. EVERYONE'S WEIRD IN THEIR OWN WAYS.

You are different from everyone else. Unless you have an identical twin, no one looks exactly like you. No one else has your style. No one else is interested in the very same things. And you know what? **You should be really proud of that.** And if anyone thinks differently, you shouldn't give a darn.

BUT THERE ARE TIMES WHEN YOU *SHOULD* CARE WHAT PEOPLE THINK

We don't get to choose what we look like or whether we find Bigfoot totally fascinating. (I can't help it! I love Bigfoot!) But there are lots of things we DO get to choose. And those are the things you should care about.

If you *choose* to be mean, and people think you're a jerk, they won't want to spend time with you. If you choose not to do your homework, and your teacher thinks you're lazy, you will get a bad grade. If you *choose* to chew with your mouth open, people will think you're gross, and they'll definitely think twice before serving you chocolate cake.

On the other hand, if you choose to kind, people will be grateful. If you choose to act brave, people will look up to you.

It's all up to you! So take care and choose carefully!

HOW TO BE BRAVE

YOU *DON'T* NEED BIG MUSCLES

When I was a kid, I was pretty sure being brave required superpowers, a uniform, and enormous muscles. That is definitely NOT the case. **Heroes are regular mortals just like you and me**. There's only one thing that sets real heroes apart: When something goes wrong, they're the ones who step forward.

YOU *DO* NEED TO BE SCARED

Being brave isn't the same thing as being fearless. Ask any hero and they'll tell you—they were scared senseless when they did the amazing thing that they did. **The fact is, in order to do something brave, you *have* to be scared**. That's what makes acts of bravery so impressive.

And you don't need to go around rescuing puppies from burning buildings in order to be a hero. Leave those feats for older heroes for now. **But I'd bet you have a chance to be brave at least once a week.**

STEP ONE: FIGURE OUT WHAT THE RIGHT THING TO DO IS

Maybe someone in your class has been accused of a prank they didn't commit. Or maybe you see someone making fun of the new kid. What would be the right things to do in these situations? If you can figure it out, you're halfway to being brave already.

STEP TWO: NOW DO IT

This is the step that separates heroes from other people. Heroes don't stand by. They go to the rescue. They know it might not be easy. They know they might make some people mad. But when they've figured out what the right thing to do is, they DO IT.

WHAT TO DO IF YOU DON'T LIKE YOUR NAME

We don't get to choose our own names. They're given to us when we're born—by people who still don't know us that well. Sometimes we're lucky and get a name we adore. But let's be honest: Things can go wrong and parents aren't perfect. Sometimes we're given names that don't suit us—or who we want to be. So what should you do if you name drives you nuts?

ADOPT A NiCKNAME

There are so many awesome nicknames available. (See the next chapter!) But getting other people to use the one you pick out can be tricky. What you'll need is a trusted accomplice. Ask a friend or family member to start calling you by your new nickname. If it's funny, ironic, or suits you perfectly, there's a chance it could take off.

Champ Buzz Kid

USE YOUR iNiTiALS

Want to sound like a president, outlaw, or children's book author? Take the first letters of your first and middle name. Now put them together. Some combinations sound cooler than others. (JK, KC, DJ, and GT, for example.) If you're lucky enough to have great initials, start using them to sign your name on all your essays, drawings, doodles, and notes.

CJ JL DY

GO BY YOUR LAST NAME

There's a good chance your friends will go along with this one—but your family probably won't go for it. (It could get a bit confusing since it's their name, too.) If that's fine by you, the best way to get this going is to start calling your friends by *their* last names. Odds are, they'll follow suit. Not only is it funny, it will make you all seem just a little bit tougher.

Jones Doodah Lee

CHANGE iT

You're 10. Unless you have a *very* good reason, it is unlikely (although not impossible) that your parents are going to let you change your name legally. But guess what? In eight short years, you'll be able to have any name you want. No one can stop you from calling yourself Dingleberry, Spiderman, or The Magnificent Trixie. (If that's really what you want.)

Sparkle Blue Zim

YOU'VE DECIDED TO GIVE YOURSELF A NICKNAME

WHAT NAME SHOULD YOU CHOOSE?

OOOH! This is going to be so much fun! The nickname you choose is going to say a lot about you. What would you like people to think?

YOU MIGHT HAVE MAGICAL POWERS

Pixie

Wiz

Merlin

Harry

YOU'RE ABSOLUTELY DELICIOUS

Nugget

Sugar

Cupcake

Tootsie

YOU KICK BUTT

Ace

Lucky

Moxie

Slick

Your Highness

NO, YOU *REALLY* KICK BUTT

Knuckles

Thumper

Boom

Spike

YOU'RE A LITTLE BIT SCARY

Boo

Chuckie

Darth

Gonzo

YOU MIGHT BITE

Mad Dog

Beast

Shark

Snake

YOU COME FROM ANOTHER PLANET

Cosmo

QOOAXR

Trust me, you are good at something. *Really* good. Possibly the best. If you're lucky, you already know what it is. But at 10, there's a good chance you haven't figured it out yet.

So how do you discover your special skill?
You're going to have to go look for it!

GET OFF YOUR RUMP

I'm sorry to report that you will never figure out what you're good at by sitting on the couch.

TRY NEW THINGS

Who knows what your secret skill is going to be? Maybe you'll end up being the best rock climber on earth. Or maybe you'll discover you make unbelievable cheese. But you won't figure it out unless you try new things.

FIND SOMETHING YOU LOVE

It's not impossible to be good at something you hate, but it's MUCH easier (and more fun) to be the best at something you love doing.

PRACTICE YOUR BUTT OFF

You won't be the best at something the first time you try it (or the first hundred times). Being the best takes time and effort. But if you love what you do, it won't seem like work!

DON'T LISTEN TO NAYSAYERS

Naysayers are people who try to bring you down. There are lots of them out there. When you meet one, ignore them. If you've found something you love, don't let anyone tell you that you can't do it.

DON'T GIVE UP

It's not going to be easy. There will be times when you want to give up. Don't! If you're going to be the best, you can't be a quitter. So keep on trying, no matter what!

WHY CAN'T YOU

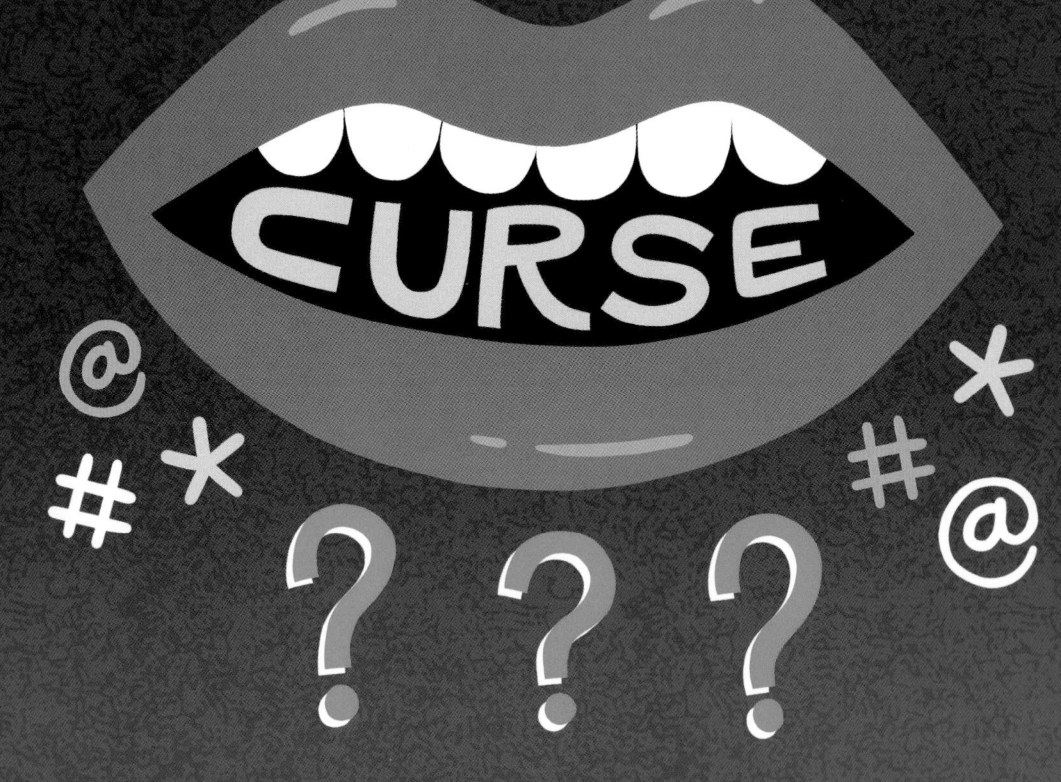

The truth is, you can. In fact, I think there's a pretty good chance that you have. (Don't worry, your secret is safe with me.) But I'd like to convice you that even though you *can* curse, at the age of 10, you probably *shouldn't*.

Why not? A lot of adults curse. Heck, a lot of kids probably curse, too. So what's the problem with saying a few dirty words here and there? Well for starters, your parents or religion might believe that cursing is wrong. I'll let your mom and dad explain why. But even if they don't care, there are some very good reasons you should keep your language clean.

YOU'LL GET IN BIG TROUBLE AT SCHOOL

See, the problem is, when people start cursing, it can be hard to stop. The more you curse in private, the more likely you are to let a bad word slip out when you REALLY don't want it to. That's the sort of thing that can get you sent to the principal's office . . . if you're lucky. If you're not, you could get into bigger trouble than that.

YOUR FRIENDS MIGHT THINK IT'S FUNNY. THEIR PARENTS WON'T

Why do you care if their parents are offended? Well, if your friends are 10, too, their parents get to decide who they hang out with. Most parents want their kids to spend time with kids who are good news. I'm sorry to report that cursing is one of the quickest ways to get yourself labeled *bad news*. Maybe that's fair. Maybe it isn't. But it will mean fewer playdates and birthday parties.

YOU'LL MISS OUT ON A LOT OF THE GOOD PARTS OF BEING A KID

If you're going to talk like an adult, a lot of people are going to treat you like one, too. And not in a good way. Kids get a lot of things that adults don't get. Lollipops. Cookies. Compliments. Piggyback rides. Start cursing like an adult and you'll start getting exactly what adults get. *Nothing*.

ONE DAY YOU'LL BE ABLE TO SAY WHATEVER YOU WANT

By then, maybe cursing won't be so tempting. But if it's something you're absolutely dying to do, it will be worth the wait. Throw a party if you feel like it! For now, enjoy the lollipops.

10 GREAT WORDS THAT SOUND LIKE CURSE WORDS

BUT (PROBABLY) WON'T GET YOU IN TROUBLE

POOP!
(WHY NOT GO WITH A CLASSIC?)

BUMFUZZLE!

URANUS!

DINGUS!

BOONDOGGLE!

SCHMUTZ!

DAGNABIT!

DINGLEBERRY!

CLATTERFART!

DIPHTHONG!

10 (REAL!) BIRD NAMES THAT MAKE GREAT CURSES

YELLOW BELLIED SAPSUCKER

BLUE FOOTED BOOBY

TUFTED TITMOUSE

GREAT BUSTARD

RED BILLED OXPECKER

LAZY CISTICOLA

HOARY PUFFLEG

TAWNY FROGMOUTH

RUFUS POTOO

TURDUS MAXUMUS
(MY PERSONAL FAVORITE)

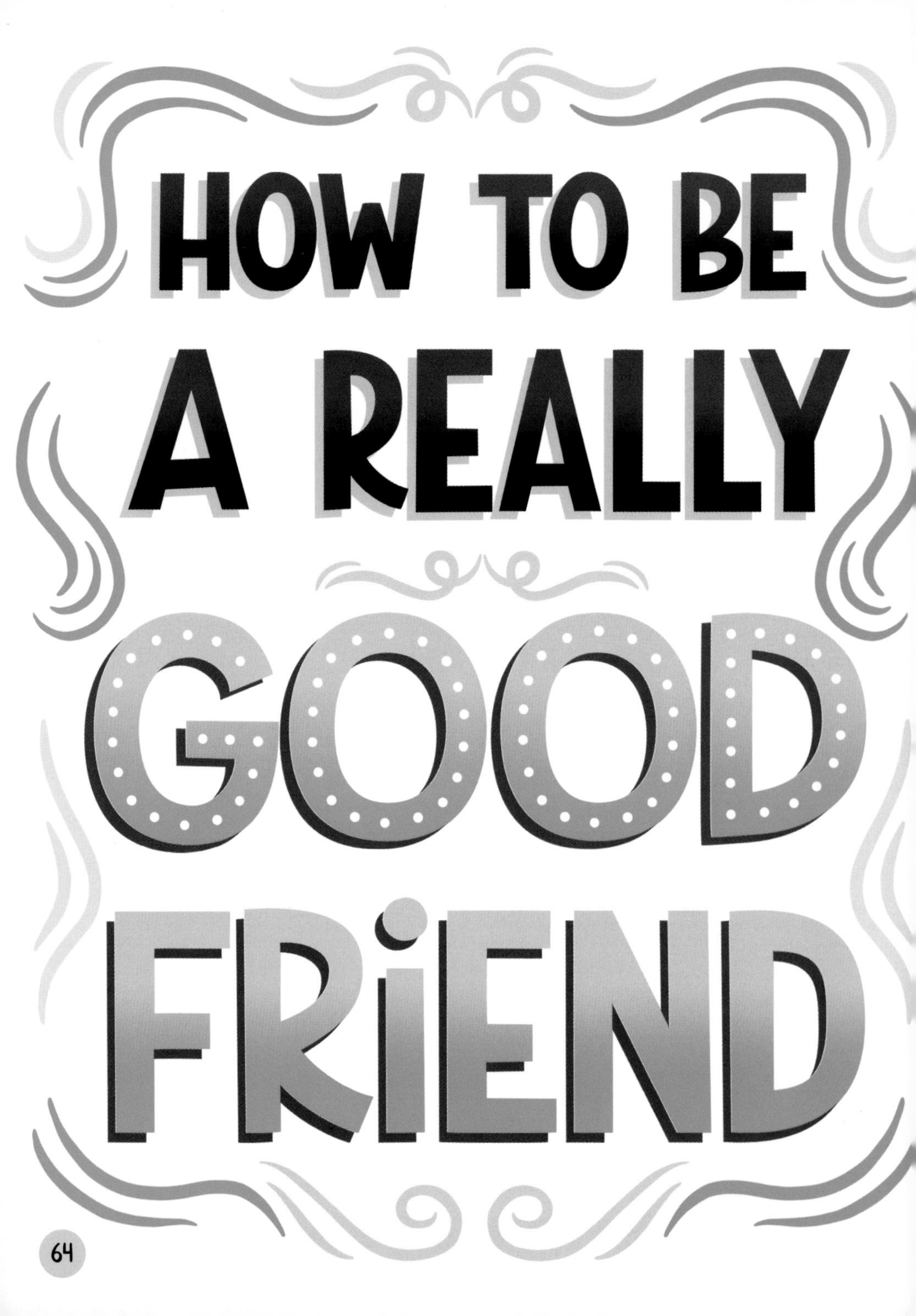

HOW TO BE A REALLY GOOD FRiEND

When you were little, friends were just kids that you played with. Now that you're 10, friends can be so much more. **A good friend is someone you trust to be there when you need a hand, an ear, or a laugh.**

Of course, none of us are perfect—and neither are our friends. Everyone gets angry, and we all argue with people we love. Some of us have even been known to throw Monopoly money up in the air when we lose a game. (Okay, that was me.) Fortunately, you don't need to be perfect to be a great friend.

DO:

- Teach them all your favorite bird names (see the last chapter!)
- Keep your friends' secrets—even the super juicy ones
- Share gum whenever you have it
- Listen when a friend needs to talk
- Have their backs—and be there when they need you
- Share amazing adventures
- Be honest—but be nice about it
- Forgive them when they say sorry (and mean it)
- Tell them if they have a booger hanging out of their nose

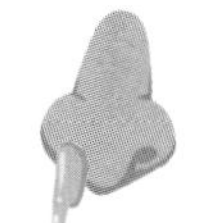

DON'T:

- Talk about your friends behind their backs
- Ask them to do something wrong (like cheat on a test)
- Expect them to always do what you want

WHY SHOULD YOU KEEP YOUR FRIENDS' SECRETS

The title of this is *why* you should keep a secret, not *how to* keep a secret. Everyone knows *how* to keep a secret—you just keep your lips shut! But a lot of us still can't manage to do it. So maybe it's time to review why keeping your friends' secrets is so important.

Your BFF just revealed the identity of his secret crush. Now it feels like the information is burning a hole inside of you! Maybe you want to climb up to the rooftops and shout the name! Or maybe you just want to whisper it in another friend's ear. Whatever urge you're feeling, you've got to resist it. And here's why . . .

FRIENDS DON'T EMBARRASS FRIENDS

It doesn't matter how silly or small their secret may sound to you. If they swore you to secrecy, the information must mean a lot to them. Sharing it with other people would be humiliating (that means *super* embarrassing). And humiliating a friend is a really good way to ruin a friendship.

SHARED SECRETS MAKE FRIENDSHIP STRONGER

We all have secrets—things we aren't comfortable telling the whole world. A true friend is someone you feel safe sharing all your secrets with. You'll know that you've found your real BFF when they never, ever laugh at you or blab your secrets to others.

IF YOU TELL SOMEONE'S SECRETS, DON'T EXPECT THEM TO KEEP YOURS

That's how it works. You give into temptation and share a secret that's not yours, and soon your secrets will be all over school, too.

HOWEVER, SOME SECRETS SHOULDN'T BE KEPT

If you know that a friend is in danger—or has been harmed in some way—you should tell a trusted adult right away.

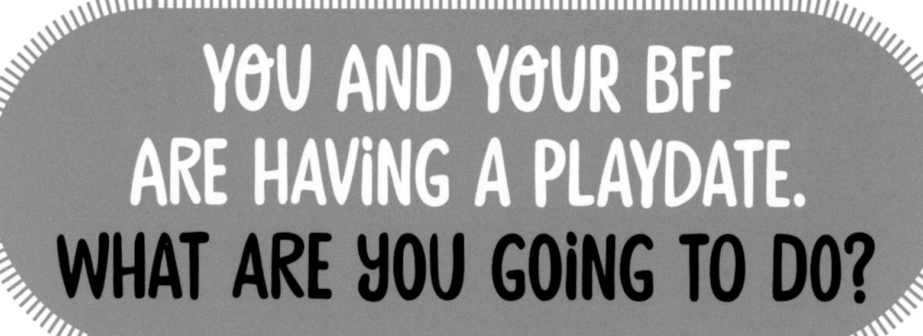
YOU AND YOUR BFF
ARE HAVING A PLAYDATE.
WHAT ARE YOU GOING TO DO?

Are you super-duper rich?
BUT OF COURSE!
NOPE
SO WHAT? The best fun is free!
WHERE ARE YOU GOING TO BE?
THE WOODS
MY YARD
THE CITY
STUCK AT HOME

LUCKY YOU!
Do you need to stick close to the house?
YES
CAMOUFLAGE HIDE 'N' SEEK
PRACTICE SURVIVAL SKILLS
I can wander around
ANIMAL TRACKING
MUSHROOM SEARCH
IS IT HOT OUTSIDE?
I'M MELTING!
Can you get your hands on a big roll of plastic?
YES
MAKE YOUR OWN SLIP 'N' SLIDE
No, but we might have two buckets
WATER FIGHT!
Meh, not really
Are there chemicals on your lawn? (Ask)
Parents say no
MAKE BACKYARD SALADS
We use weedkillers or pesticides
BEETLE RACES!
HAS ANYONE EVER CALLED YOU "HAWK-EYED"?
THAT'S MY MIDDLE NAME!
How do you feel about rats?
They are nature's superheroes!
RAT WATCHING
Don't make me barf
GREEN-MAN HUNT
Perfect vision is not one of my super powers
Ok, have a camera?
YEP!
BEST THING CONTEST
NOPE
SECRET SECRET AGENTS
CAN YOU USE THE KITCHEN?
YES!
How about the stove?
Oh yea, I'm super mature
RICE KRISPIE MONSTERS
My parents don't understand me
FOOD-COMBO CHALLENGE
NOT YET
Do you have more than one bath?
YEP!
BATHROOM BEACH VACATION
NOPE
DISGUISE FASHION SHOW

BACKYARD SALADS

See page 110.

CAMOUFLAGE HIDE-AND-SEEK

Don't run and hide. Stay near your house and use your best camouflage skills to blend in with your surroundings.

MAKE YOUR OWN SLIP 'N SLIDE

Take your big roll of plastic and spread it out on the yard. The longer your slide, the better! Add a little dish soap, turn on a hose, and get the whole slide nice and wet.

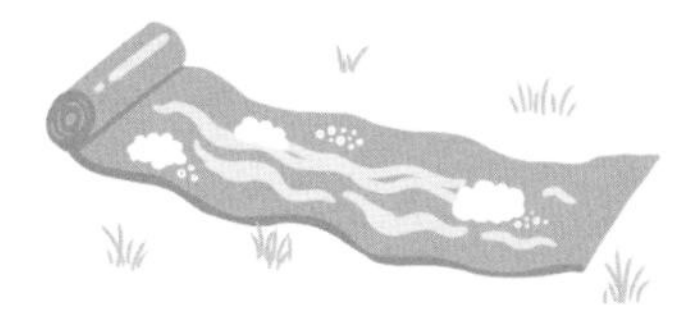

SECRET SECRET AGENT

This is a great game to play in crowded places. Pretend there's a bad guy/gal out there, and you two have to find them. But here's the thing—it's probably someone no one would ever suspect. Figure out who it is, what they're planning, and how to deal with them—all without ever letting them know you're watching.

BEETLE RACES

See page 119.

RAT WATCHING

Yeah, they're gross, but they're also pretty awesome. And if you live in a city, they're all around you. Do not try to touch them or make friends!

BEST THING CONTEST

Take your cameras and go for a walk. Each person must snap ten photographs of things they think are amazing (or super gross or whatever you're into). At the end of the walk, have a third person choose a winning photograph!

GREENMAN HUNT

They're carved into buildings all over most cities, but most people never see them. Greenmen (and sometimes women) are faces that look like they're made out of plants or leaves. Some of them are pretty creepy. Once you spot one, you'll start seeing them everywhere! (You may even wonder if they're watching you.)

RICE KRISPIES MONSTERS

See page 29.

FOOD-COMBO CHALLENGE

Read the next chapter!

ANIMAL TRACKING

Grab a guide to animal footprints. There are creatures all around you—and you can find them if you know how to look.

MUSHROOM SEARCH

Looking for mushrooms can be an awesome scavenger hunt. Look, but don't touch or taste!

BATHROOM BEACH VACATION

Run a bath. Get into your bathing suits. Make some fancy drinks and put on some relaxing music. Dip your toes in the water and pretend you're on holiday.

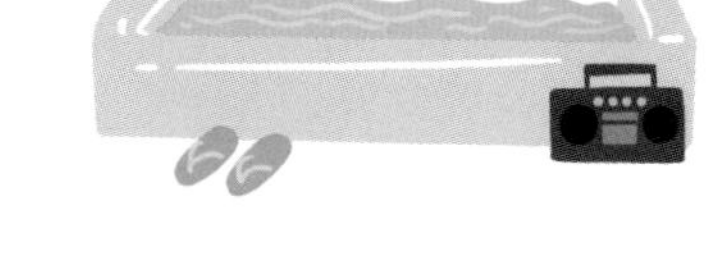

DISGUISE FASHION SHOW

Come up with new ways to disguise your appearance. Then put on a show for your family and see if they know who is who!

PRACTICE SURVIVAL SKILLS

Pretend you're stranded on an island for the night. Make a shelter and find things to eat!

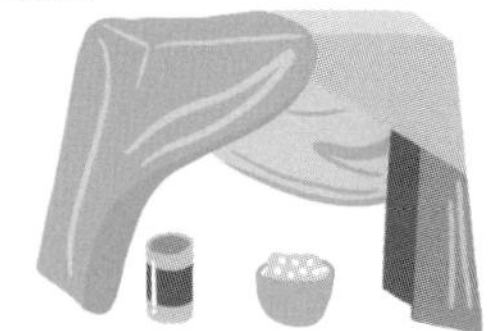

WATER FIGHT

Buckets (or plastic cups) are really all you need, but feel free to add squirt guns and water balloons to your arsenal.

PLAY THE FOOD-COMBO SANDWICH GAME!

Get twelve index cards, sticky notes, or other small squares of paper. Separate them into THREE PILES.

On the cards in **PILE #1**, write down the following condiments:

KETCHUP

MAYONNAISE

JELLY

PEANUT BUTTER (IF YOU'RE ALLERGIC TO PEANUTS, MAKE IT HONEY OR MUSTARD)

On the cards in **PILE #2**, write the following vegetables/fruits:

PICKLES

AVOCADOS

BANANAS

TOMATOES

On the cards in **PILE #3**, write the following ingredients:

CHEESE (ANY KIND)

POTATO CHIPS

MEAT (SALAMI, HAM, ETC.)

LAST NIGHT'S LEFTOVERS

If you're missing an ingredient, just replace it with something you have in the fridge.

Each person must close their eyes and choose one ingredient from each pile. Then they must make a sandwich using those ingredients and **EAT IT**. NO WASTING FOOD!

WHAT TO DO WHEN SOMEONE DISAPPOINTS YOU

Have you ever felt like someone really let you down? Maybe they weren't there when you needed them—or did something they shouldn't have done.

It stinks when people disappoint us. Unfortunately, you're going to be disappointed again. Probably pretty soon. Your friend might forget your birthday. Your mom might not be able to make it to your big performance. Your teacher might give you a grade you don't think you deserve. Things that seem totally unfair are going to happen to you throughout your life.

Here are a few things to keep in mind when you're disappointed:

SOMETIMES PEOPLE CAN'T HELP IT

If your mom couldn't make it to your performance because she had to work, she's probably pretty sad about it, too. Ask yourself whether the person who disappointed you could have done anything differently. If the answer is no, feel free to be mad at the world. Go to your room and scream into your pillow if you need to. But don't be mad at that person.

PEOPLE SCREW UP

Maybe they could have done something differently. Nobody's perfect. The most wonderful people in the world make mistakes. That includes you. You're going to disappoint people from time to time. Even people you love. So if the thing that's happened isn't so bad, why not give the person a break? Accept their explanation or apology and forgive them. Bonus: If you do, they're more likely to forgive *you* when you disappoint *them*.

DECIDE HOW LONG YOU'RE GOING TO BE UPSET

When my feelings get hurt, I decide how long I'm going to be sad (or mad). If it wasn't such a big deal, I may stay sad for ten minutes. If it was something terrible, I might be upset for a day or two. But that's it. I set an alarm to go off, and when my time to be sad is up, I do my best to let it go.

IF THE SAME PERSON KEEPS DISAPPOINTING YOU, DO SOMETHING ABOUT IT

Talk to the person and tell them how you feel. Give them a chance to change. If they don't, look for people who make you feel safe and happy—and learn to rely on them.

OH NO! SOMETHING TERRIBLE HAPPENED! HOW LONG SHOULD YOU STAY UPSET?

This is really up to you! But here's what I recommend.

Failed a test

Dropped your ice cream cone

Bike stolen

Little sister kicked your butt at Scrabble

She's 9

She's 3

Wanted waffles, got eggs

Got a hideous haircut

Hats are your friends

Best friend won the award you wanted

Didn't get into Harvard

Extraterrestrials have invaded your town

Seem nice

Really bossy

Broke my leg

5 MINUTES

Don't waste any more time. Go study for the next one!

10 MINUTES

Stay upset any longer and you'll miss your chance to investigate

ARE YOU KIDDING? 0 MINUTES!

Friends are more important than awards

HALF DAY

Doing something brave

ALL DAY

Doing something dumb

WHEN TO DUMP A FRIEND

There are plenty of 10-year-olds who are friends with kids they've known their entire lives. They played together as babies, and now they're still hanging out . . . even though they're not sure they want to be friends anymore.

FUN FACT!

When I was a kid, they used to make us sing a song that went something like, "Make new friends, but keep the old. One is silver and the other gold." Maybe you got lucky and that song went out of fashion before you made it to preschool. The point is, the song is wrong. Sometimes old friends are gold. And sometimes they're completely rotten.

There is no rule that says you have to be friends with the same people your entire life. In fact, it's pretty likely you'll need to give a few friends the boot. Here are some very good reasons to break up with a friend:

THEY'RE MEAN

To you or to other people. Or animals. Or people who work in restaurants. Or anyone, really. Life is way too precious to spend time with people who are mean.

THEY MAKE YOU FEEL UNWANTED

Do you have a "friend" who often makes you feel left out? They'll invite everyone to a pool party—but you. Or when they're picking players to be on their team, they won't pick you. Anyone who does this is not your friend. Move on.

THEY LIE TO YOU—OR ABOUT YOU

It's important to have friends you can trust—and it's hard to trust people who can't be honest. A fib here and there isn't something to get upset about. But if you know someone who lies all the time or makes up stories about you, that's a really good sign that they aren't a good friend for you.

THEY CONSTANTLY GET YOU IN TROUBLE

A little trouble is fine. I'd even say healthy! (Don't quote me on that.) But at the age of 10, you shouldn't be hanging out in your principal's office every day. And you definitely shouldn't be spending time with the local police.

WHAT TO DO WHEN LIFE ISN'T FAIR

I'm sure you've been told that life isn't fair.
That's true. It isn't. Far from it.

When it comes to little things, I'd advise you to suck it up. But when something happens that's SO unfair that you don't think you can live with it? DON'T. There are things you can do to make the world a better, fairer place. Yes, even when you're 10 years old. In fact, *especially* when you're 10 years old.

SPEAK UP

When you see something unfair, don't stay quiet. Speak up. Do it politely but powerfully.

STAND UP FOR THE LITTLE GUY

Is there someone who's being treated unfairly and isn't able to stand up for themselves? Stand by their side. (This is also a good way to make a friend for life.)

STAND UP FOR YOURSELF

And do not be afraid to ask for help if you need it.

FIND A WAY YOU CAN HELP

Is something happening in the world that you don't think is fair? Find an organization that raises money to fight the problem. Or start one yourself!

SHOULD YOU TEXT, CALL, OR VISIT?

You've got something to say. Maybe it's "Sorry" Maybe it's "Happy Birthday!" Whatever the case, you have at least three ways to say it. You could call the person you need to reach, visit them in person, or you could be lazy and just send a text. What's the best thing to do?

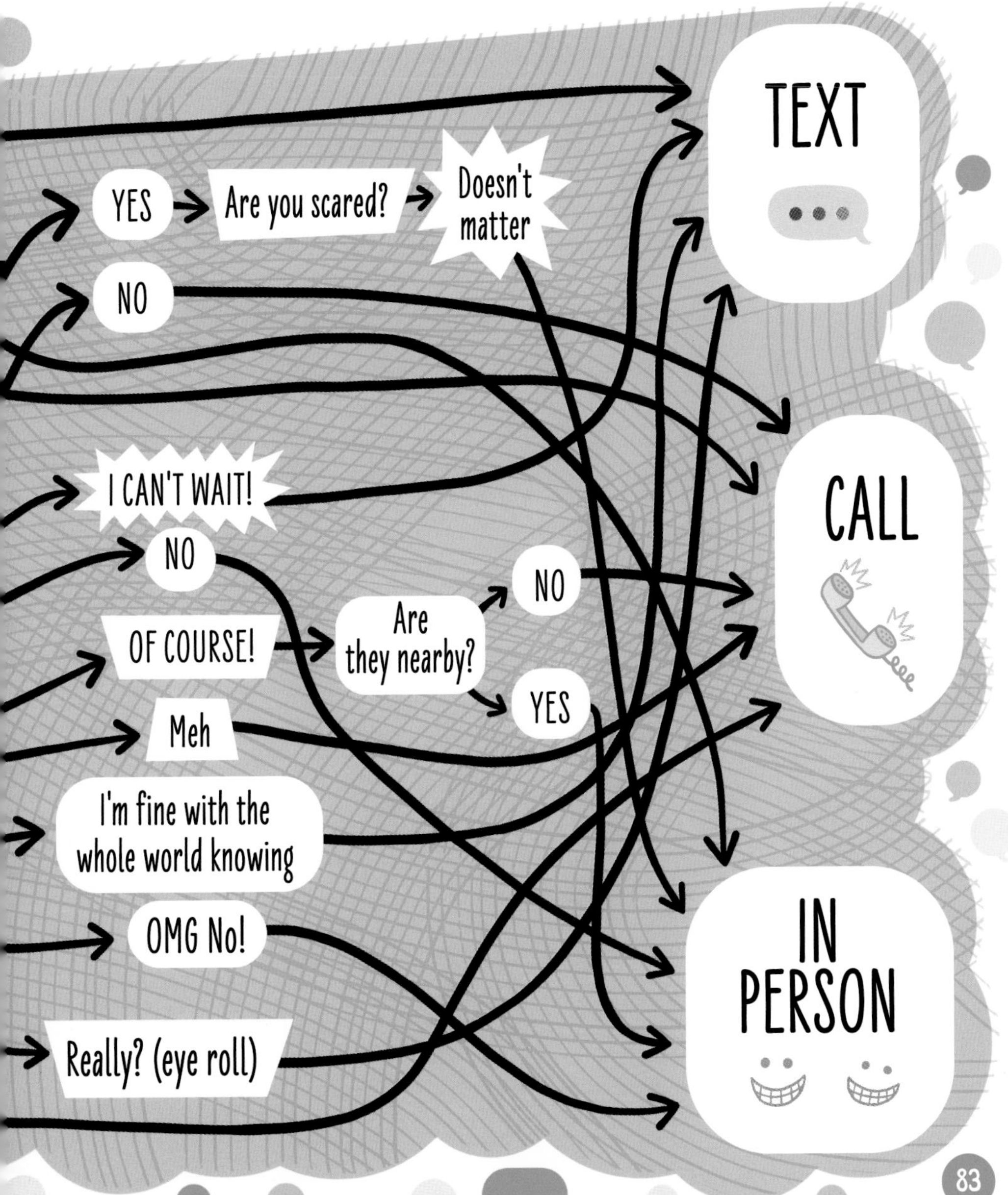

HOW TO DEAL WITH A MEAN TEACHER

Most teachers are wonderful human beings who deserve medals for spending their days with a bunch of rowdy 10-year-olds. Mean teachers aren't very common. But sadly, they do exist. (Boy did I learn that lesson the hard way in fifth grade!)

What should you do?

Well that depends on just how "mean" your teacher is!

"Sorta mean" isn't really mean in my book (and this is my book)! It usually means a teacher is strict and doesn't put up with any funny business. My advice to you in this situation is . . . get used to it, buddy. It's probably a good thing he/she isn't letting a bunch of 10-year-olds go nuts in school.

This is a teacher who can be quite unpleasant at times. Maybe they yell just a little too loudly. Or they're quick to punish you for even the teensiest crimes. You will definitely come across a teacher like this at some point in your life. Being around them isn't going to be fun, but there's not much you can do about it. Consider it good training. You're going to meet a LOT of people like this in your life.

Okay, this is when things start getting bad. A teacher should never insult kids. Or smack them. Or go out of their way to make kids feel bad or dumb. Or punish kids in cruel ways. If you have a teacher like this, tell your parents—even if it's another kid who's being picked on. Adults can be bullies, too, and bullies must be stopped. Make sure you take action!

WHAT IF A TEACHER HAS IT IN FOR YOU?

I've been in that situation, my friend. And let me tell you, it is not fun. Always be polite. Do your homework. Do your best to stay out of trouble. But don't let them get the better of you either. Stand strong! Keep a record of the things they do! (Make sure you list time, date, and witnesses.) Tell your parents about the situation. And if it gets bad enough, don't be afraid to take your case to the principal.

HOW TO LEARN SOMETHING REALLY IMPORTANT

Maybe you have a big test coming up. Or maybe you just want to impress someone with your giant brain. You have a lot you need to learn—and a short time to learn it. How can you cram all those facts into your head?

MAKE A SCHEDULE

If you can avoid it, don't try to learn everything in one day. Try to spread out your study time over a few days, if possible. Make sure you schedule breaks in between. Your brain needs time to absorb everything you've learned! Even if you can learn everything super fast (in one day), you are more likely to forget it that way—your brain can't handle it all at once!

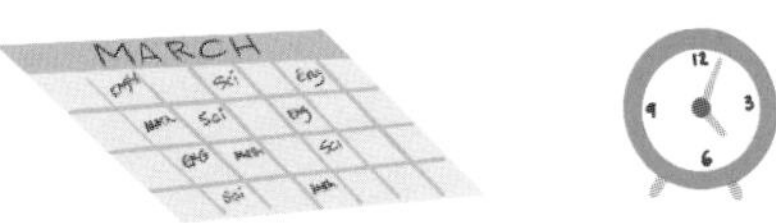

FIND A PLACE WHERE YOU CAN FOCUS

Some of us (like me) need absolute quiet. Others need a little noise in the background. Find out what works for you!

TURN OFF YOUR SCREENS

Seriously. There is nothing on YouTube that's going to help you!

PRETEND YOU'RE THE TEACHER

After you've read everything you're supposed to read, put the book down. Now pretend you're a teacher and try to explain what you've learned to someone else!

ASK FOR HELP IF YOU NEED IT

If there's something you don't understand, don't panic. Talk to your teacher (or a parent or a sibling) and ask them for a little help.

10 QUESTIONS THAT WILL MAKE FIELD TRIPS FASCINATING

Now that you're 10, you're starting to learn about things that happened a long time ago. You've probably been on a few field trips to places that looked old and dull.

When I was your age, I thought history was boring. Now it's my all-time favorite subject. That's because I now know just how dirty, disgusting, and exciting the olden days were! Tour guides may try to avoid all the gross stuff, if you want to find out about it, you'll have to ask the right questions!

Here are a few questions to ask the next time you visit a historic place:

1. What did the people who lived here eat that no one eats anymore?
2. Where did they go to the bathroom?
3. What did they do with their poop?
4. What did they do with the dead?
5. How did most people die back then?
6. What were the most common diseases?
7. What was life like for kids my age?
8. How did they punish their criminals?
9. What did people wear and how did they get dressed in the morning?
10. What scared them the most?

Some of these questions may seem silly at first, but I promise you that they're not! For example, knowing what people did with their poop tells you a lot about their lives. Until the twentieth century, most people didn't have toilets in their houses. So they'd poop in a special pot they kept under the bed. (Sounds fun, right?) When they were done, sometimes they'd throw everything out the window! See how fascinating history can be?

HOW TO ENJOY WRITING

Around the fourth grade, kids begin writing their first social studies or history papers. Choose your subject wisely, and the assignment can be super fun. (No, seriously.) And you will learn all sorts of incredible facts that will astound your friends and family. (No, seriously.) So what kind of subject would you like to write about?

DISGUSTING

SURPRISING

Is the world's biggest pyramid in Egypt?

Could women be Viking warriors?

Where is the first emperor of China buried?

How did the Egyptians make their mummies?

A SOCIAL STUDIES PAPER

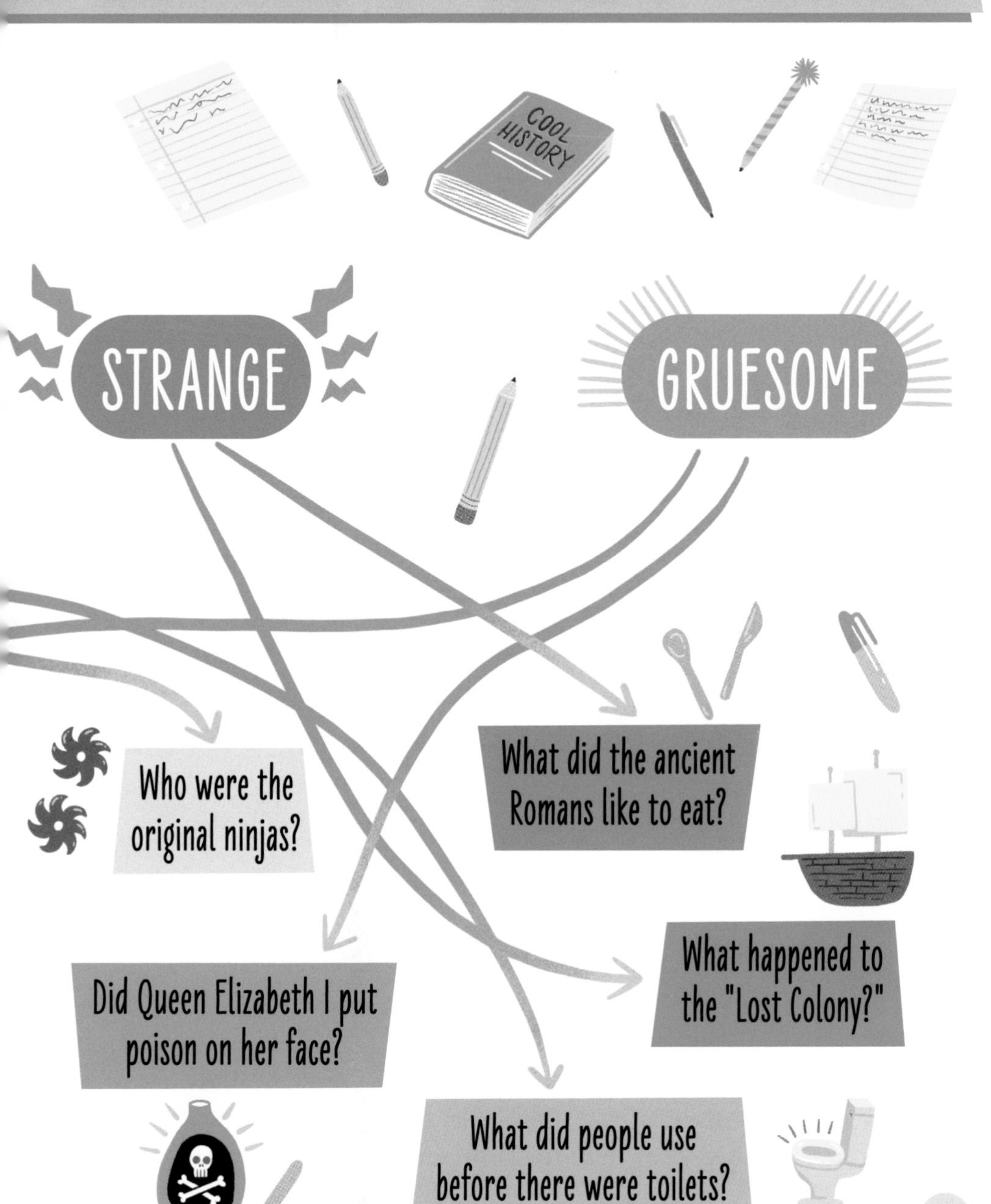

HOW TO STAY SAFE ONLINE

You should avoid email and social media for as long as possible, but at some point in the next few years, you will probably be allowed to create your own accounts. This is a huge responsibility!

The internet can be a dangerous place for kids. That's why your parents may not want you to have your own accounts yet. When the time comes, here's how to stay safe:

NEVER, EVER, EVER SHARE YOUR PASSWORDS WITH ANYONE BUT YOUR PARENTS

This is super important. Do not give your passwords to your friends—or to anyone online who claims they "need" them. No one should be able to get into your accounts except you, your mom, and/or your dad.

NEVER CHAT WITH ADULTS— OR KIDS YOU DON'T KNOW

We talked about this last year, but it's important to repeat! You've probably been told a million times not to chat with adults on the internet. But don't chat with kids you don't know either. There's always a chance they're adults pretending to be your age.

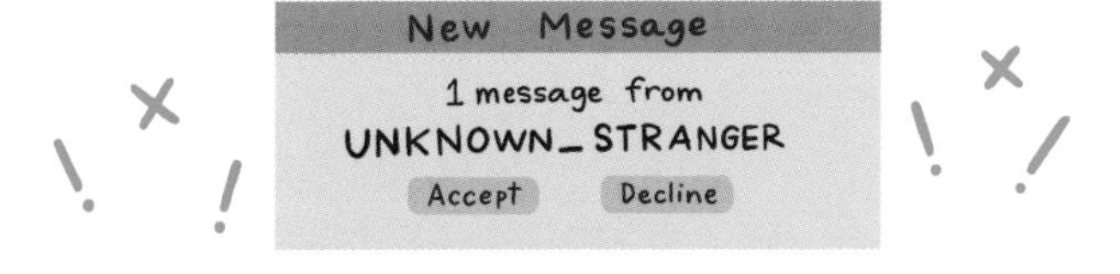

REMEMBER—NO ONE ONLINE SHOULD EVER TELL YOU TO *DO* ANYTHING

It doesn't matter what they want you to do—DON'T. Don't take pictures if people ask you. Don't visit sites they want you to visit. If someone is trying to get you to do something, it is a *very* good sign that they're bad news. Block them immediately and move on.

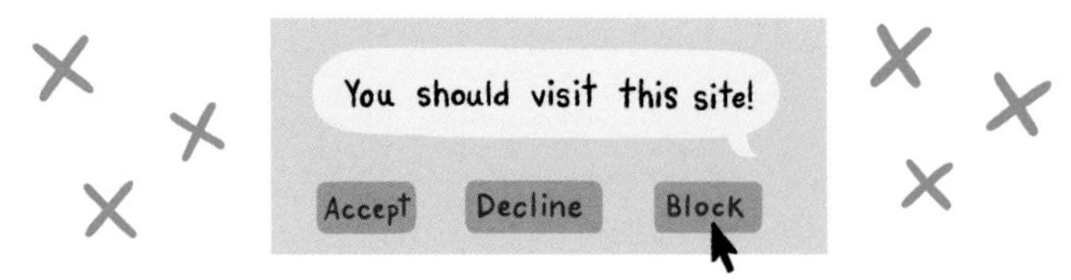

NEVER POST PHOTOS YOU WOULDN'T WANT YOUR GRANDMA TO SEE

In fact, never even *take* any photos that you'd be ashamed to let the whole world see. You know why? Because these days, there's a very good chance that the whole world *will* see them.

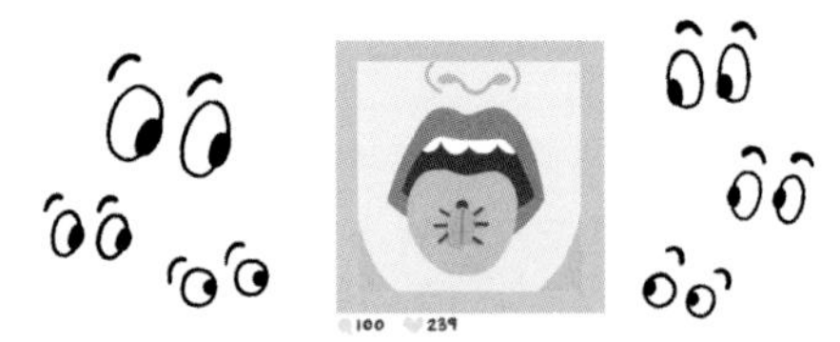

DON'T WRITE ANYTHING YOU WOULDN'T SHARE WITH YOUR PRINCIPAL

What's true for pictures goes for the messages you send to your friends as well. If you have a secret you wouldn't want everyone to know, do not write it down. And be careful what language you use. Foul language may make your friends giggle, but their parents (and yours) probably won't be amused.

MAKE SURE ALL OF YOUR SOCIAL MEDIA ACCOUNTS ARE SET TO PRIVATE

No one should see your posts or pictures but your friends and relatives. Do not invite anyone you don't know well to be your friend online. Even if the person claims to be a kid, you'll never know if it's true. Treat everyone you meet online like a stranger—because that's exactly what they are.

BLOCK BULLIES—AND DON'T BE ONE YOURSELF

Sometimes when people are online, they think they can get away with things they'd never try in real life. They say mean stuff. They poke fun at other people. If someone does this to you, block them immediately. Do not give them a second chance. And if you're the one doing it, don't be surprised if you get blocked, too. Even when you're online, you should always treat people the way you would want to be treated.

KEEP IN MIND—NOT EVERYTHING YOU SEE ONLINE IS TRUE

You're probably going to be doing research for school this year. Find out which sites are trustworthy and stay away from the rest.

WHAT TO DO IF YOU'RE FOLLOWED

One of the best things about being 10 is walking places by yourself. But before you lace up those sneakers and set off on your next adventure, make sure you know what to do if you think someone is following you. I don't want you to be scared. I want you to be *prepared*.

KNOW YOUR ROUTE

A route is the path you take from one location to another. You probably walk to the same spots several times a week—school, the library, a friend's house, or the park. The next time you set out, look for safe places along your route. A safe place is somewhere you can run if you need help. It could be a store, a restaurant, a police station, or a friendly neighbor's house. Keep a list of safe places in your head in case you ever need one.

PAY ATTENTION

Don't walk with loud music playing in your headphones. Make sure you know what's going on all around you. Whenever you can, stick to streets where there are lots of people.

REMEMBER THE RULES ABOUT STRANGERS

Do not stop to talk to adults if you're by yourself. Do not let anyone touch you. If someone grabs you, go completely nuts. Scream, kick, and bite if you have to. And never, ever, ever get into anyone's car.

IF YOU THINK SOMEONE MAY BE FOLLOWING YOU, DON'T TAKE ANY CHANCES

Follow the instructions below right away. Don't wait! You might be wrong, but take action anyway. It's better to be safe than sorry!

IF YOU'RE BEING FOLLOWED BY SOMEONE IN A CAR

Spin around and RUN in the opposite direction. The car won't be able to turn as quickly as you can. Book it to the closest safe place and immediately call the police.

IF YOU'RE FOLLOWED BY SOMEONE ON FOOT

RUN as fast as you can to a public safe place—like a store or restaurant. Don't be afraid to scream and shout. Call the police and don't leave until they arrive.

TELL A TRUSTED ADULT

This is important. If you were followed by someone, you need to let people know. It doesn't matter if you were somewhere you weren't supposed to be—or doing something you weren't supposed to do. If someone was following you, they could end up following other kids. Make sure the police know who to look for.

WHY YOU SHOULD ALWAYS LISTEN TO YOUR GUT

"Listen to your gut"?
What the heck does that mean?

Your gut is your belly. And no, it doesn't talk. But if you listen, it can tell you a lot.

Sometimes when you come across a person or a place or a situation that just doesn't feel right, your belly will start to feel a bit queasy. Your heart may race. You can't figure out exactly what's wrong, but your gut is telling you something's not right. **Why should you listen?**

YOUR GUT HAS A SUPERPOWER

It's called intuition, and you should always trust it. If your gut tells you that someone is bad news, stay away from them. If your gut tells you that a place might be dangerous, don't go there. And if you're in a situation where your gut is telling you something bad might happen, hit the road as soon as possible.

How does it work? No one knows for sure. **But listening to what your gut tells you is one of the most important ways to keep yourself safe.**

HOW TO SCARE THE PEE OUT OF SOMEONE

This trick may be crazy simple, but it works like a charm. Please use it for good, not evil. There's a big difference between having fun and terrorizing innocent people.

STEP ONE: GATHER SUPPLIES

You won't have to round up many supplies for this prank. **All you need is a set of walkie-talkies.** (Two phones will work nicely, too.) Make sure the walkie-talkies are on and the batteries are charged. **Then place one of the walkie-talkies under the person in question's bed.**

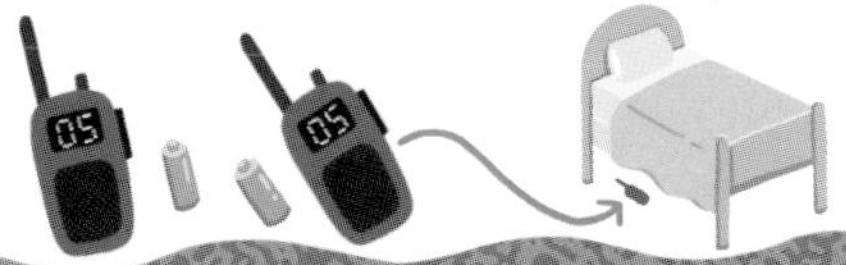

STEP TWO: BE PATIENT

Now wait. The best time to act is a couple of minutes after they've crawled into bed and turned out the lights. But don't wait long enough for them to fall asleep!

STEP THREE: GET CREEPY

At just the right moment, begin making super creepy sounds. What kind of creepy sounds, you ask? Well that's up to you! I think hearing someone whisper my name from beneath the bed would definitely send me running and screaming out of the room. You have lots of terrifying options, of course. Come up with your own or choose from the handy list below!

Only pull this prank on someone who's likely to think it's funny once they've recovered from their terror! And don't be surprised if one of your walkie-talkies gets confiscated.

HOW TO TERRIFY YOUR PARENTS AND GROW A ZOMBIE TENTACLE

In my opinion, this is the greatest project of all time. It's easy, cheap, and unbelievably gross.

THINGS YOU'LL NEED:

A wire hanger

Cotton filling, cloth scraps, or toilet paper

Plastic wrap

A small paintbrush

Mod Podge (or regular white glue)

Round cereal with a hole in the middle (like Fruit Loops or Cheerios)

Three gross paint colors

A devilish imagination

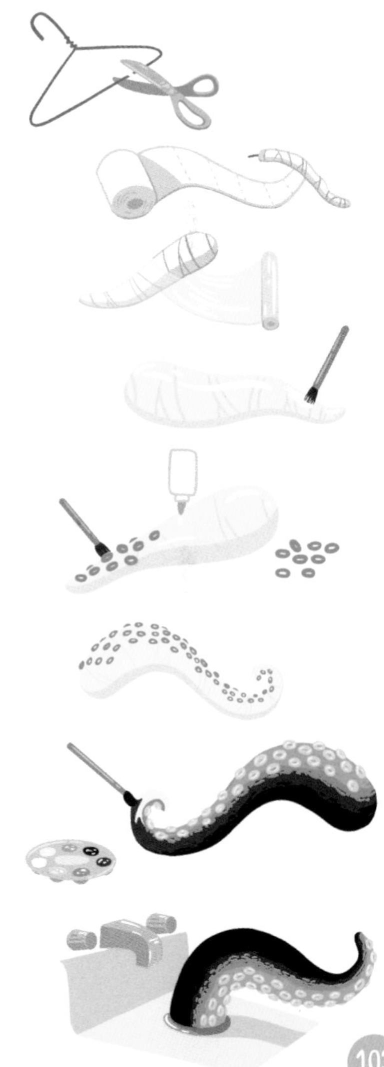

1. Get an adult to help you snip a bit of wire hanger that's at least 8 inches long.
2. Wrap the cotton, cloth, or toilet paper around the piece of wire hanger. Make it thicker on one end and thinner on the other (like a tentacle).
3. Now, wrap your plastic wrap around the covered wire until everything's nice and tight.
4. Using your paintbrush, cover the entire thing in a layer of Mod Podge (or white glue mixed with a little water) and wait for it to dry.
5. Dab a little glue on your Fruit Loops and stick them to one side of your tentacle, making two rows down the entire length. (These are your suckers!) When you're done, paint another layer of Mod Podge over everything and let your tentacle dry.
6. Before you paint, bend your tentacle into a creepy, curly shape.
7. Paint it colors that you think are scariest. (Black, gray, and green are good choices.) Make the top side of your tentacle one color, the underside another color, and the suckers a third!
8. Now (heh heh) find a place to put it! Your zombie tentacle will look great creeping out from under the toilet seat, emerging from a sink drain, or growing out of something that's been left in the fridge!

HOW TO SEND SECRET MESSAGES

You've got something you need to write down and send to a friend, but you don't want the whole world to see it. How can you pass a note that no one but you and your friend can read?

MAKE SOME INVISIBLE INK

Making invisible ink is super simple, easy, and best of all, almost totally FREE! First, find a white sheet of paper and something to write with. A small paintbrush or a Q-tip will work perfectly. Got it all? Awesome. **For your invisible ink, you can use lemon juice, milk, vinegar, soapy water, sugar water, or . . . no joke . . . pee!** (But don't use pee. That's gross.) Write out your message on the paper. When the person gets the note, all they need to do is hold it up to a warm lightbulb or radiator and the message will be revealed!

GET YOUR HANDS ON A BLACK LIGHT

Secret messages are just as easy to send using an ultraviolet black light. You can find little ones in hardware stores (where they are definitely not free). Be careful not to stare into the lightbulb—it can hurt your eyes! **You'll also need a different kind of ink if you're using a black light. Clear laundry detergent or tonic water are prefect.** (Snot will work, too, but I don't recommend it.) The letters will be invisible until you shine the black light on them!

MAKE IT TINY

Inside most pens and Magic Markers, you'll find a space that's just big enough for a tiny scrap of paper. Untwist your pen or pop off the end of your Magic Marker. **Write your note using the smallest letters possible.** Then roll it up and hide it inside your pen or marker. Let your friend "borrow" your writing utensil and recover the note inside.

WRITE IT ON A BANANA

This is a good trick to play on your family. **In the morning, take a pin and write a secret message into the skin of a banana.** Then give the banana to your mom/dad/sister/brother for lunch. During the day, the letters will turn brown, and your message will slowly be revealed!

HOW TO USE A CIPHER

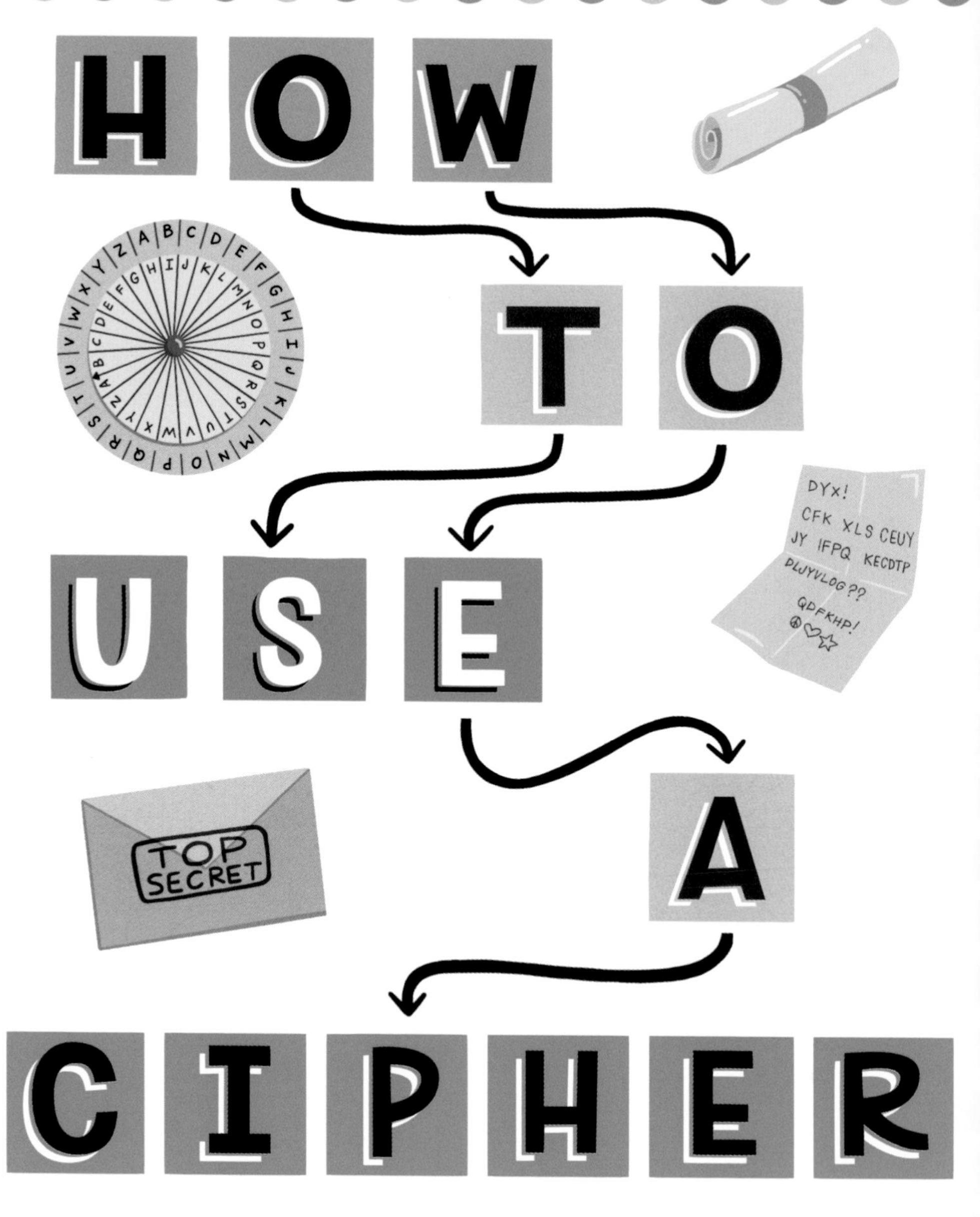

One of the most popular ways to send a secret message is to use a cipher.

There are many different kinds of ciphers,
but the easiest to use is a substitution cipher.

1. Pick a keyword. Make it a simple word with no repeated letters. Let's say our keyword is **FARTY.** (Because that's how I roll.)

2. Write out the alphabet in a straight line. This is your "plaintext" alphabet:

A B C D E F G H I J K L M N O P Q R S T U V W X Y Z

3. Your "ciphertext" alphabet will go right beneath it. The letters FARTY will take the first five places. Remove those four letters from the rest of your ciphertext alphabet:

A B C D E F G H I J K L M N O P Q R S T U V W X Y Z
↓ ↓
F A R T Y B C D E G H I J K L M N O P Q S U V W X Z

4. When you write your note, substitute your plaintext alphabet for the ciphertext alphabet. In this case:

WHATS UP? Becomes **VDFQP SM?**

5. Make sure your friend knows the keyword so they'll be able to decipher it!

HOW TO WALK LIKE A NINJA

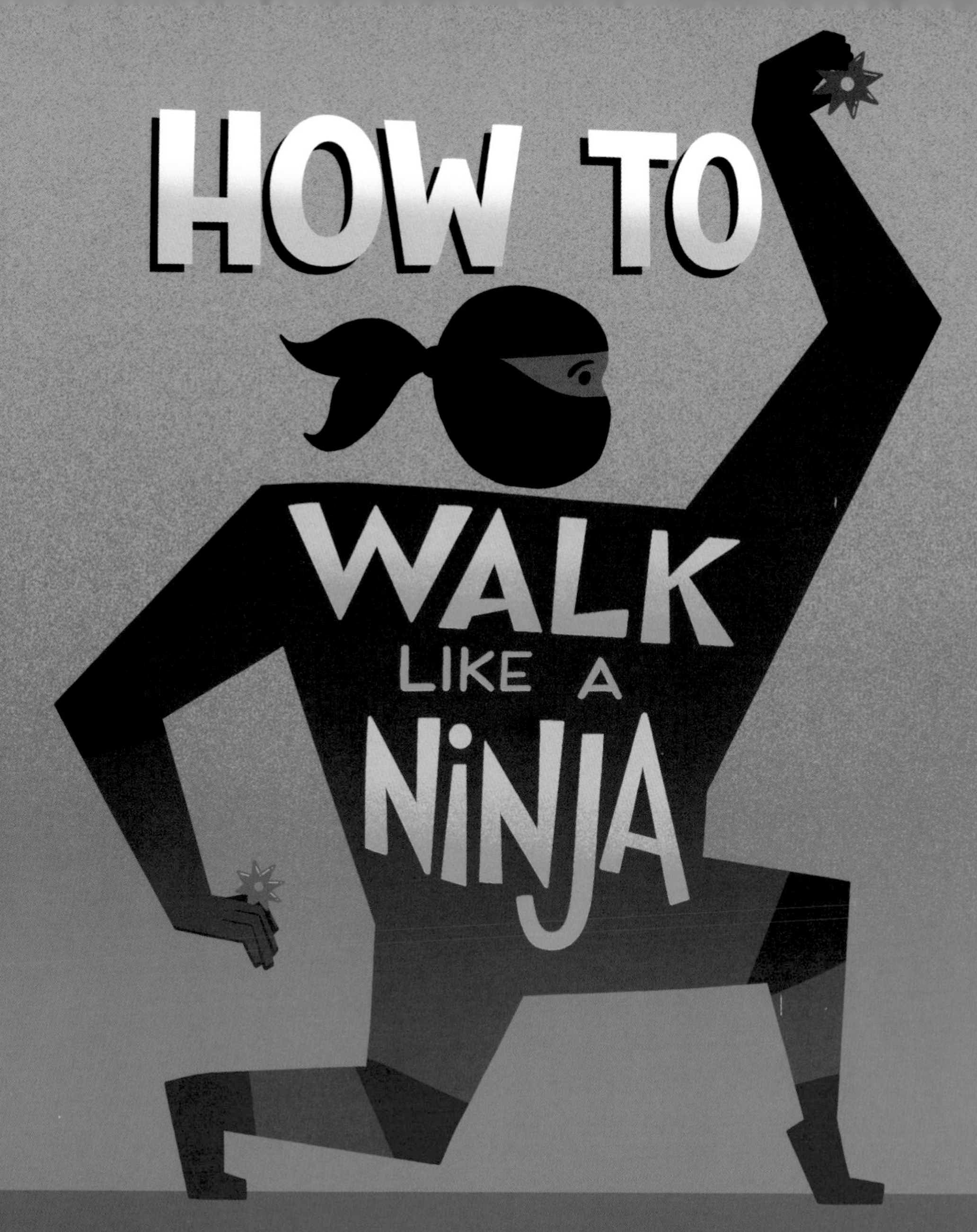

Some of you may grow up to be ninjas. Most of you will not. (Don't get upset. There are lots of other cool things to be.) But no matter what you become, being able to walk like a ninja is sure to come in handy.

How do ninjas walk? Veeerrry quietly. They can sneak up on you before you know it—and sneak away before they get caught. **Skills like these are useful for many reasons.** (Reasons I'm sure I don't need to explain!)

Here's how to do it:

LISTEN TO YOUR HOUSE

Early one morning, before the rest of your family gets out of bed, walk through your house with your ears open. Listen for floorboards that creak or stairs that groan. Remember where the noisy parts are so you can avoid them later.

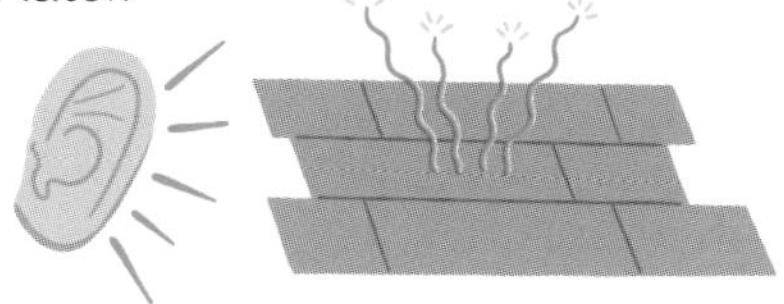

WALK HEEL TO TOE

If you thump your whole foot down each time you take a step, you're always going to get caught. Put your heel down first and slowly lower the rest of your foot until your toes reach the ground. (Obviously this is a lot easier if you're wearing socks or shoes with soft soles.)

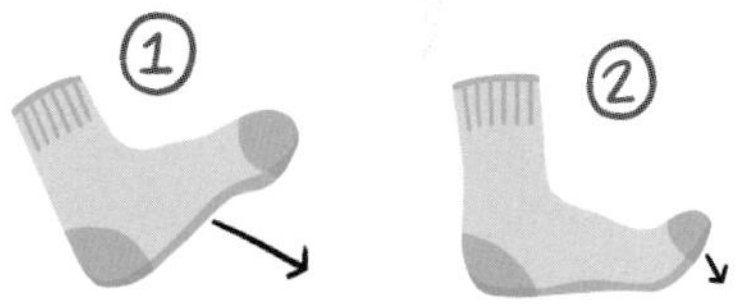

STAY CLOSE TO THE WALLS

If there are places in your house where the floor makes tons of noise, try walking next to the wall. The boards won't creak as much there.

TAKE IT SLOWLY

Once you've done your research, start building your skills. Take your time—there's no need to rush—and watch the ground for anything (toys, pets, whoopee cushions) that might make a racket.

MATCH STEPS

If you're sneaking behind someone who's walking, make sure to put your feet down when they do. If you match their steps, they won't be able to tell yours from their own!

HOW TO MAKE A BACKYARD SALAD

If you're lucky enough to have a backyard (I'm not), you probably have everything you need to make a great salad! Lots of the plants we call weeds are not only edible, but tasty, too. Add a few edible flowers and you'll have the most gorgeous salad you've ever seen.

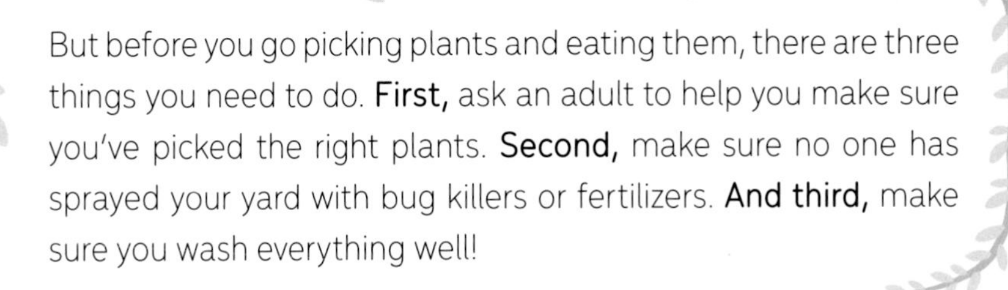

But before you go picking plants and eating them, there are three things you need to do. **First,** ask an adult to help you make sure you've picked the right plants. **Second,** make sure no one has sprayed your yard with bug killers or fertilizers. **And third,** make sure you wash everything well!

PLANTAIN

Yes, there's a type of banana that's called a plantain. But we're talking about something else altogether. The type of plantain you'll find in your yard is a "weed." Pick a few of the smallest leaves and rip them into small pieces.

DANDELION

You can eat any part of the dandelion! Add a few leaves to your salad. Sprinkle a few little yellow petals on top!

KUDZU

I hope you don't have kudzu in your backyard, but where I grew up, a lot of people do. It's a vine that takes over everything! But if you can get your hands on a few leaves, they'll taste great in your salad. The purple flowers are yummy, too.

RED CLOVER

The leaves are edible, but go for the flowers. They're sweet and have a great crunch.

VIOLETS

Violets are the perfect finishing touch for your salad. But don't pick them out of anyone's flower garden!

ONIONS

Wild onions will add flavor to any backyard salad. They look and taste a lot like the scallions you can buy—so have a good look at some scallions the next time you're at the grocery store. Then see if you can find similar-looking plants outdoors!

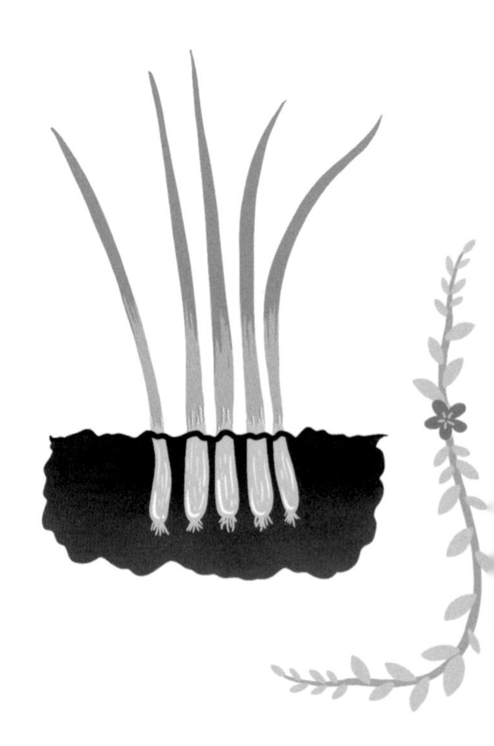

PRICKLY PEAR CACTUS FRUITS

Not all backyards have grass and trees. If you're a desert-dwelling kid, see if your backyard is home to a prickly pear cactus. The fruits the plant produces are very tasty. **(Weird fact: Prickly pear cactus fruits are called tuna.)** Just be sure to peel them before you chow down! Like the rest of the plant, the fruits are covered in mean little spines.

WHY YOU SHOULD EAT MORE BUGS

OK, I'm just going to come right out and say this: If you haven't eaten a buy by the age of 10, you haven't really been living.

Seriously? You've never eaten a bug? Not even a little ant—just to see what it tastes like? Well, this is something we'll need to fix right away. Why? I can think of a hundred reasons! But today I'll offer you five.

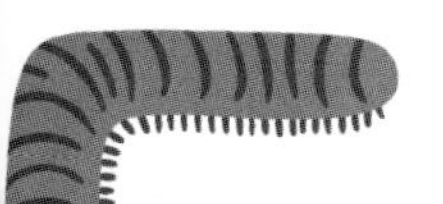

BUGS ARE DELICIOUS

Don't believe me? Then ask (almost) every other country in the world. The French eat snails, which they call *escargot*. Parts of Mexico are famous for their grasshopper tacos. In Thailand, you can buy scorpions on a stick! Can you imagine how delicious bugs must be if everyone on earth wants to eat them? We're the ones missing out!

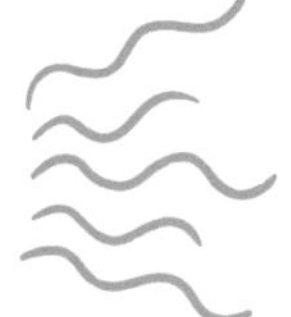

THEY'RE PACKED WITH ENERGY

I bet at some point a coach, teacher, or doctor has told you to make sure you eat lots of protein. Well, you know what? **Bugs are FULL of protein.** They're also low in bad stuff like sugar. They're practically the perfect snack!

THEY'LL MAKE YOU MORE INTERESTING

Allow me to me explain. Eating bugs won't make you more interesting. Being the kind of person who doesn't gag at the thought of eating bugs *will*. It's called having an open mind. **People who are willing to try new things lead fascinating lives.** People who refuse to eat anything but chicken nuggets probably won't.

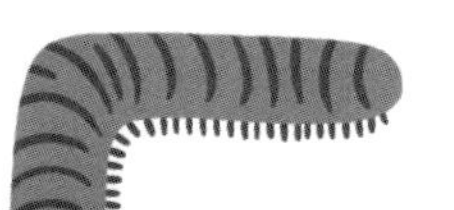
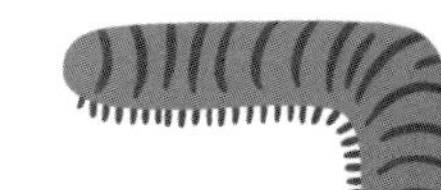

YOU'LL HAVE PLENTY TO SNACK ON IF YOU GET LOST IN THE WOODS

I'll be honest, I don't spend a lot of time in the woods. But if you're the kind of person who does, I recommend getting to know all the edible bug species out there! If you're ever lost, a handful of beetles and a few dozen earthworms could mean the difference between life and death!

IF YOU CAN'T FIGHT THEM, EAT THEM

Yes, bugs are often annoying. Can you think of a better reason to eat them? Some of the most annoying of all also happen to be quite tasty. Stinkbugs, for example, are despised by everyone—except for the people who've discovered how tasty they can be with a little salt and pepper!

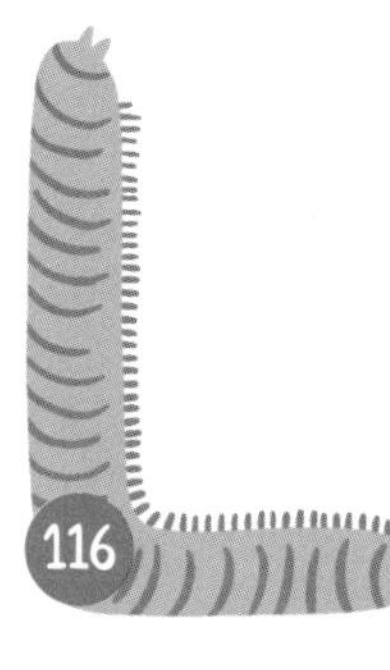

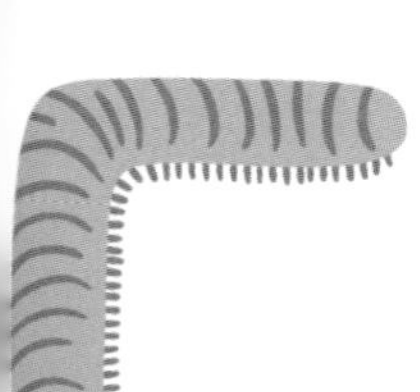
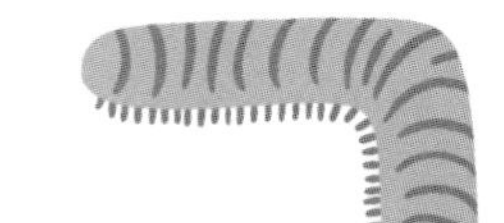

BUGS YOU SHOULD TRY (JUST MAKE SURE THEY'RE COOKED!)

Crickets and grasshoppers
(great crunch)

Mealworms
(nice and nutty—but perfectly safe for those with nut allergies)

Earthworms

(squeeze out the poop before you put them in your mouth)

Ants and termites

BUGS YOU SHOULD AVOID

Anything that's brightly colored or hairy

Snails or slugs
(though escargot from a nice French restaurant is divine)

HOW TO HAVE FUN WITH THE BUGS YOU DON'T EAT

Maybe you'd rather play with bugs than eat them. That's great, too!

BEETLE RACES

Beetle races are more fun with a friend (or sibling) or two. All you have to do is make a racetrack with a starting line and a finish line. Then go out and collect the fastest-looking beetles you find. Set them all down at the starting line and see which one crosses the finish first! (Beetles that fly away are disqualified, but it's totally acceptable to encourage your beetle to eat the competition.)

BEETLE BATTLES

If you are lucky enough to live in a part of the world where giant rhinoceros beetles and Hercules beetles thrive, then you can stage beetle battles! They're super popular with 10-year-olds in Asia, particularly Japan. (There are cool videos on YouTube. Ask a parent to find them.)

1. Find or adopt a Hercules or rhinoceros beetle. Here in the United States, you'll probably have to find one. In Japan, you can get them from vending machines!

2. Convince your friends they need beetles as pets. This shouldn't be hard. They're pretty awesome.

3. Get a large twig and put it inside your beetle tank. The twig should be just big enough for two beetles to come face-to-face.

4. Put two beetles on the log.Watch them battle like gladiators. The one that throws the other one off is the winner!

If your bug is the champion, give it a nice piece of fruit as a special treat!

A GREAT 10-YEAR-OLD PRANK

THE MAGICAL CHICKEN

You mastered fake spiders back when you were 8. Now you're getting old enough for some cool, complicated pranks! This is one of my all-time favorites!

THINGS YOU'LL NEED:

6 eggs
A safety pin
White glue
White tissue paper
Shiny paper

STEP ONE: MAKE TWO HOLES IN YOUR EGG

This is so much fun. Use the safety pin to make a tiny hole in the top of your egg. (Be careful! You don't want to break the shell.) Then turn the egg upside down and make a bigger hole at the bottom. Make it the size of a gumball—and don't worry if it doesn't look 100 percent perfect.

STEP TWO: BLOW THE EGG OUT OF ITS SHELL

Put your lips to the smaller hole and blow the egg out of its shell and into a bowl. (For those of you who've never done this before, yes, it is totally possible.) DO NOT waste the raw eggs. They can still be eaten! (FYI: Scrambled eggs is a delicious dish many 10-year-olds enjoy making!) When your eggshell is empty, wash it out and let it dry well. While it's drying, put a dab of white glue on the smaller top hole to seal it. Leave the bottom hole open.

STEP THREE: MAKE YOUR FAIRY DUST

Cut your shiny paper up into teensy tiny pieces. (Any kind of colored paper is fine to use. But shiny paper feels much more magical.) When you're done, roll a scrap of leftover paper into the shape of a funnel. Insert the bottom of the funnel into the eggshell and pour in your confetti until your eggshell is half full!

STEP FOUR: SEAL IT UP

Cut a piece of the white tissue paper that's just bigger than the remaining hole in your egg. Use the white glue to seal the hole with the tissue paper. Let it dry well.

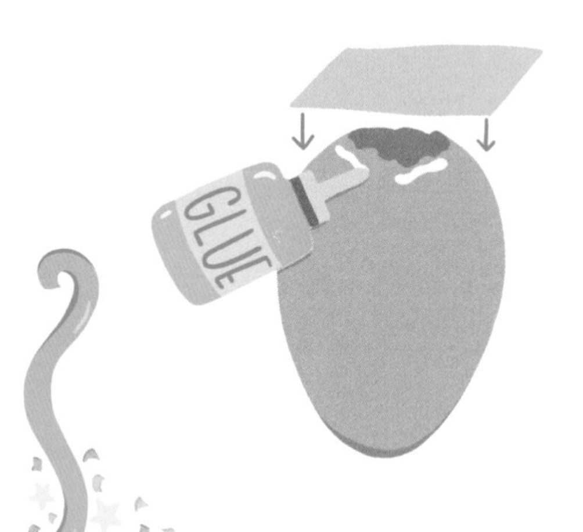

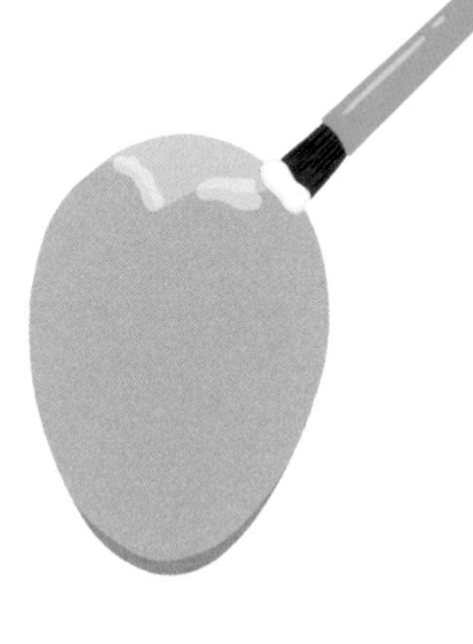

STEP FIVE: **HAVE YOUR EGGS GO UNDERCOVER**

Once you have six dry eggs that are filled with fairy dust, put them back in the carton. If the tissue-covered holes are facing down, your eggs should look like regular old chicken eggs.

STEP SIX: **AMAZE YOUR FRIENDS**

Show the carton to your favorite friend/sibling/gullible adult and tell them it's filled with very rare, magical eggs. When they refuse to believe you, take them outside, pull out one of the eggs and throw it at a tree. The egg will burst in an amazing cloud of sparkly paper! (Not up for making 6 magical eggs? You can also make a single egg and pretend to "find" it outside.)

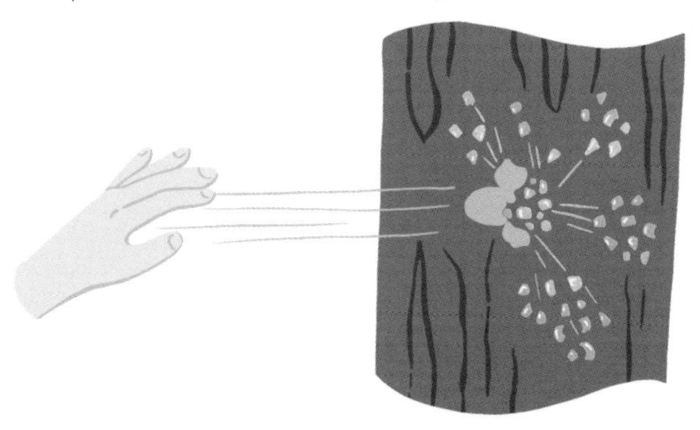

DON'T THROW YOUR EGGS AT PEOPLE.

Little pieces of eggshell aren't good for their eyes.

THE EASIEST 10-YEAR-OLD PRANK: FAKE VOMIT

I don't know why you would ever want to make fake vomit. It's so unbelievably disgusting! No one wants to look at something like that! (heehee)

If you're going to use your fake vomit more than once, you might want to invest in the plastic variety. You can usually buy it at novelty stores for a couple of bucks. But most of us only really need fake vomit once or twice a year at most.

When that special day rolls around, here's your answer:

VEGETABLE SOUP

There's a very good chance you have a can in your cupboard right now. It doesn't matter what kind it is. Chunky, reduced sodium, or the kind with letters made out of pasta—it all works. Now don't run to the kitchen and use it right this second. Let it sit there. You'll want to save it for the right moment. (Believe me, you'll know when the right moment arrives.) When you're ready . . .

1. Open the can.
2. Mush it up with a fork.
3. Pour where needed.

YOU'RE WELCOME!

SOME FUN THINGS TO DO WHEN YOU'RE NOT IN PUBLIC

Now that you're 10, it's time to start acting more mature in public. But don't worry! Growing up doesn't mean you can't continue to have gross, silly fun with your friends!

As a matter of fact, you can keep having it no matter how old you get! If you're lucky, the gross, silly fun will never end! So find a nice quiet spot, and . . .

FART WITH YOUR ARMPiTS!

1. Pick your favorite hand. Make sure it's clean and dry.
2. Raise the opposite arm, cup your hand, and place it over your armpit. Make sure your hand is pressed down against your armpit. You should feel a little bit of air in the middle of your palm
3. Bend your arm and pump it up and down.
4. When that little bit of air gets pushed out from under your palm, it should sound like a nice, juicy fart.
5. Enjoy, my friend. Enjoy.

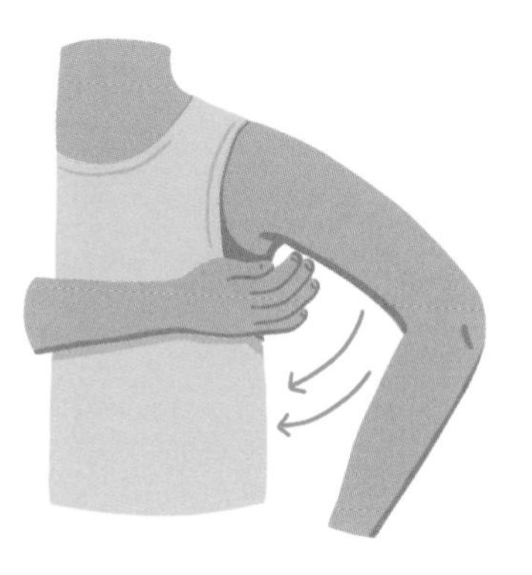

OR:

- Make your friends shoot drinks out their nostrils!
- Burp the national anthem!
- Eat snacks without using your hands!

YOU'RE 10. DO DISGUSTING STUFF WITH YOUR FRIENDS!

BUT IT'S TIME TO STOP ACTING LIKE A BARBARIAN WHEN YOU'RE OUT IN PUBLIC.

Why? If you gross everyone out, you might not get invited to go many places. All that stuff you got away with when you were little? Now that you're 10, it's not going to fly. So are you a barbarian in public? You might be if you answer yes to any of the following . . .

- [ ] I SHOW EVERYONE WHAT'S IN MY MOUTH WHEN I EAT.
- [ ] I EAT MY BOOGERS.
- [ ] I MAKE BIG MESSES AND LEAVE THEM FOR OTHER PEOPLE TO CLEAN UP.
- [ ] I SMELL LIKE POOP.
- [ ] I BELCH AT THE TABLE.
- [ ] I BLOW MY NOSE ON MY SHIRTSLEEVE (OR ANYTHING OTHER THAN A TISSUE).
- [ ] I DON'T FLUSH THE TOILET.
- [ ] I DROP MY TRASH ON THE GROUND.
- [ ] I HAVE TEMPER TANTRUMS.
- [ ] I SHOUT IN RESTAURANTS AND STORES.
- [ ] I PEE ON BATHROOM SEATS.
- [ ] I "DOUBLE-DIP."
- [ ] I DON'T SAY "THANK YOU" WHEN SOMEONE DOES SOMETHING NICE FOR ME.
- [ ] I DON'T COVER MY MOUTH WHEN I COUGH.
- [ ] I DON'T SAY "PLEASE."
- [ ] I SAY MEAN THINGS ABOUT THE WAY PEOPLE LOOK.
- [ ] I HOLD MY FORK LIKE A SHOVEL.
- [ ] I PEE IN POOLS.

Oh, come on! **Do you really need 10 reasons?**

You're 10 years old. You mastered the art of urination YEARS ago! You know where to pee and not pee. (Do pee: toilets, bushes, the great outdoors. Do not pee: bed, on other people, and POOLS.) But if you need to be reminded, here's why shouldn't you treat pools like giant toilets . . .

1. **Pools can't be flushed.** The pee doesn't go away. Oh no. It stays in the pool until the pool is drained. You know how often that happens? NOT VERY OFTEN. Do you want to swim in a pool filled with pee? Even if it's your own?
2. If you think it's okay to pee in the pool, your friends will, too. Think about that for a minute. **I know you like your friends, but do you like them enough to SWIM IN THEIR PEE?** No, you do not. So make sure everyone knows it's not okay.
3. Yes, people put a chemical called chlorine in pools to help kill germs. But if the chlorine is busy dealing with your pee, there might not be enough to kill all the germs.
4. When pee combines with chlorine, it makes a gas that can cause problems for people with asthma. And you know what? It's not good for you either. Seriously!!!
5. **YOU ARE NOT THAT LAZY.** There is definitely a bathroom close by. If not, there's probably a really nice bush.
6. If people find out, they may not want to swim with you. (I mean, come on, can you blame them?)
7. **It's gross.**
8. **It's really gross.**
9. **It's really, really gross.**
10. **OMG IS IT GROSS!**

A COUPLE MORE THINGS TO KNOW:

YES you should shower before getting into the pool. Your body is covered with germs. Wash them off so the chlorine doesn't have to do so much work!

NO there is no such thing as a "urine detector." Your pee will not turn blue in pool water. Why am I telling you this? BECAUSE YOU ARE OLD ENOUGH TO DO THE RIGHT THING!

So you're looking to make big bucks, are you? Awesome. I admire your initiative! The day you can whip out a hard-earned five-dollar bill and buy your mom a cup of coffee will be one of the greatest days of your life.

What? You aren't going to spend your cash on coffee for your mom? I wish you could see me shaking my head right now. Oh well, it's your money, and you can spend it however you like. That's the whole idea, right? Unfortunately, you won't be able to work for a company until you're 14. But there are quite a few ways for enterprising 10-year-olds to haul in some cash.

EXTRA CHORES

You're 10. You should be helping out around the house. Maybe your parents give you an allowance in return. If so, lucky you. Look around and see if there are other chores that need to be done. If you agree to do extra work, you may be able to negotiate a raise.

START YOUR OWN BUSINESS

If you live in a place where lots of people walk by every day, stands of all sorts can be very successful. Lemonade stands are the classic choice. Selling bottles of water on hot summer days can be smart, too. But why not hot cocoa? Or cookies? Or Rice Krispies treats (page 26)?

MAKE STUFF AND SELL IT

When my sister was in grade school, she realized she could make better friendship bracelets than everyone else. So she started selling them to her friends and classmates. She got "rich," and I was green with envy. Is there something you can make that other people might want to buy? It's never too early to become an entrepreneur!

ODD JOBS

Not everyone has parents who give them an allowance. (Mine certainly didn't!) If you're like I was, look for jobs in your community. You're probably too young for babysitting, but you can walk dogs, take care of pets when your neighbors are on vacation, rake lawns, weed flowerbeds, or teach old people (those over 20) how to use their phones and computers. VERY IMPORTANT! Do not accept any jobs unless your parents know your new boss and approve of the work you'll be doing.

BUSKING

What's busking? It's when you perform in public and put out a hat so people passing by can put money inside. You gotta have serious guts for this one. (And a permit in some cities.) And don't do it without taking an adult along with you. (Seriously. There are a lot of weird people out there.) Most buskers sing and dance. But if you have a talent for magic tricks or telling jokes, why not see if you can go pro? (Take advantage of being young and cute while you still can!)

HOW TO BABYSIT YOUNGER KIDS

It won't be long before you're old enough to babysit. (It's not really an age thing. It depends on how responsible you are.) Babysitting can be a great way for girls and boys to make money of their own. But you have to take it very seriously. If you're not sure you're ready, wait until you are.

If you're serious about babysitting, you should take a first aid class and find out how to perform the Heimlich maneuver (if a child is choking) and CPR (if a child stops breathing). This is stuff you should learn anyway! Here are a few other things you should know:

LITTLE KIDS LOVE DANGER

You cannot take your eyes off a little kid. I'm not exaggerating. The second you look away, they'll be climbing the curtains or throwing themselves down the stairs. Honestly, it's a miracle most kids ever make it to kindergarten. So don't plan on reading books or playing video games while you're babysitting.

LITTLE KIDS AREN'T GREAT WITH TOILETS

You may end up changing diapers or wiping butts. And let me tell you, depending on what the kid's eaten, it can get pretty nasty. I hope you're cool with that. (Your parents call this "payback.")

LITTLE KIDS WILL EAT ANYTHING

Again, not joking. If you aren't paying attention, they could end up eating cat poop, laundry detergent, or a whole tube of Chapstick. You'll need to know what to do if they end up choking—and what number to call if they swallow something poisonous.

LITTLE KIDS ARE CUTE AND THEY CAN BE REALLY FUN

Okay, enough of the scary stuff. If you like little kids, babysitting can be fun. You'll probably get to play with a bunch of toys you forgot you loved. (If you don't like little kids—and not everyone does—find another way to make money.)

HOW TO MAKE SURE YOU NEVER MISS A THING

This year, you've got places to go and people to see. If there's something super important coming up that you absolutely cannot miss no matter what, here's what you need to do:

SET AN ALARM

Parents aren't perfect. (I know this comes as a HUGE surprise to you.) If you have to get up early on the big day, don't trust them. Set your own alarm! Heck, set TWO alarms if it's that important. In fact, you know what? Go ahead and set as many as you like.

WRITE IT DOWN ON YOUR CALENDAR

You should have a paper calendar hanging on your wall where you will see it a million times a day. Yes, I know there are calendars on computers and phones, but nothing beats an old-fashioned calendar with a DON'T FORGET!!!!!! message written on the right date.

IF YOU USE A DIGITAL CALENDAR, SEND YOURSELF REMINDERS

Every time you add a new calendar entry, you should be able to send yourself a couple of alerts or reminders so you don't forget. I always schedule one reminder the day before the event—and another one a few hours before.

GET BACKUP

Tell at least one other person about anything you really don't want to miss. If your alarms, calendars, or reminders fail, there's always a chance a human brain could save you. But now that you're 10, you should try to rely on yourself!

HOW TO ACCOMPLISH SOMETHING ABSOLUTEY ENORMOUS

So there's something big you need to do. Maybe it's something you really, really want to do. (Like building a treehouse.) Or maybe it's something you've been dreading. Whatever it is, it's sooooo big that every time you think about it, you feel sick. You can't figure out how you're going to do it!

Have you found yourself in this situation yet? If not, you will. The next time you do, I want you to ask yourself one simple question: What's the best way to eat an elephant?

The answer: bite by bite. Get it? It's much easier to conquer tasks that seem big and terrifying if you break them down into bite-size bits. (Please don't eat elephants. They're wonderful creatures.)

FIRST, SET A DEADLINE

A deadline is the time when something HAS to be done. If it's schoolwork, your teacher will probably set the deadline. If it's something you want to do outside of school, you'll have to decide for yourself when you want to be finished. Ask people who might know how long it will take. Give yourself plenty of time. But stick to your deadline!

CUT UP THE WORK INTO BITE-SIZE BITS

Make a list of all the things—big and small—you will need to do to finish your project. For example, if you need to write a three-page book report, you will need to:

Find a good book

Read each chapter

Figure out what you want to say

Make an outline of your essay

Write page one

Write page two

Write page three

If you'd prefer a more exciting example, let's say you're going to build a treehouse. Here's what you would need to do:

Find a good tree

Figure out how your treehouse can fit in the tree

Make a drawing of what it will look like

Have someone handy make sure your design won't fall down or blow away

Make a list of the stuff you'll need

Collect your supplies

Learn how to use any tools you've never used before

Make a work schedule

Start working (the number of days you'll need depends on your design)

Have the handy person check your work every day

Decorate your finished treehouse

Enjoy the greatest secret lair a 10-year-old can have

When you look at each of the parts, it doesn't seem very hard at all. It may take a few weeks, but you can get it done!

DO A LITTLE EVERY DAY

You'll be amazed by how easy it is to accomplish something huge if you do just a little bit every day. And because you won't feel rushed or stressed out, you'll be less likely to give up!

HOW TO SAVE THE WORLD

Yep, that's right. You can save the world. "But I'm 10!" you say. That's okay. It's never too late to get started! (JK)

You've probably heard that our planet is in trouble. Humans need to take action immediately before things get any worse. All over the globe, kids just like you are stepping up to save the day.

There are thousands of ways for kids to help. I couldn't even begin to list them all! But here are a few ways to get started . . .

FIND OUT WHAT'S GOING ON

Ask a teacher or a parent to help you find information on climate change, endangered species, pollution, and other important environmental subjects. You may end up knowing more than a lot of adults! Be sure to share what you learn with your friends and family.

JOIN A CLUB OR START YOUR OWN

You may read about something that really bugs you. I can guarantee there are other kids out there who feel the same way! Look for an organization that's devoted to helping fix the problem. If you can't find one, start your own! At my neighborhood school, the kids have started their own club to raise money to help save endangered species. Every dollar makes a difference!

JOIN A MARCH

Maybe you've seen photos or videos of huge crowds marching to encourage governments around the world to take action. Those crowds are made up of people like you. Each and every person makes them bigger, louder, and more likely to be heard.

CLEAN UP YOUR ACT

There are lots of things you can do at home to help the environment. You've probably learned about them in school. Don't waste water. Use as little plastic as possible. Recycle everything that you can. It may not seem like much, but if every kid did what she or he could, it would make a huge impact!

LEARN MATH

Nope, that's not a joke. You know who will find solutions to our planet's problems? Scientists. There are a million different kinds of scientists, and they all study different things. But there's one thing all of them need to know—math. If you're not good at math, you can find lots of other ways to save the world. But if you are, think of math as your superpower and find a way to use it!

HOW TO AVOID WASTING YOUR PRECIOUS TIME

If you want to save the world or accomplish something amazing, you're going to need to get busy! You can't waste precious time on any of the following things!

TRYING TO MAKE FRIENDS WITH SOMEONE WHO DOESN'T LIKE YOU.
(THEIR LOSS!)

HANGING AROUND WITH PEOPLE WHO AREN'T NICE.

PRETENDING TO BE SOMEONE YOU'RE NOT.
(UNLESS YOU'RE UNDERCOVER OR IT'S HALLOWEEN.)

WHINING AND TEMPER TANTRUMS.
(ANNOYING PEOPLE IS NOT A GOOD WAY TO GET WHAT YOU WANT.)

LYING.
(IT'S WRONG—AND ODDS ARE YOU'LL GET CAUGHT IN THE END.)

TRYING TO GET "LIKES" ON SOCIAL MEDIA.
(MAKE FRIENDS IN REAL LIFE!)

TRYING TO TEACH A DOG HOW TO USE A HUMAN TOILET.
(TRUST ME.)

SPENDING ALL DAY IN FRONT OF A SCREEN.

STAYING MAD FOREVER.

PLAYING DUMB SMARTPHONE GAMES.

TRYING TO IMPRESS EVERYONE.

MINDING OTHER PEOPLES' BUSINESS.
(UNLESS YOU'RE INVESTIGATING A CRIME.)

FOUR GOOD REASONS "LIKES" ARE DUMB

You're 10, so there's a chance you know more about social media than a lot of adults. You probably know that many sites let you "like" posts by clicking on a little heart or a thumbs-up sign. A lot of people care about how many likes they get. But they shouldn't!

THEY'RE A TRiCK

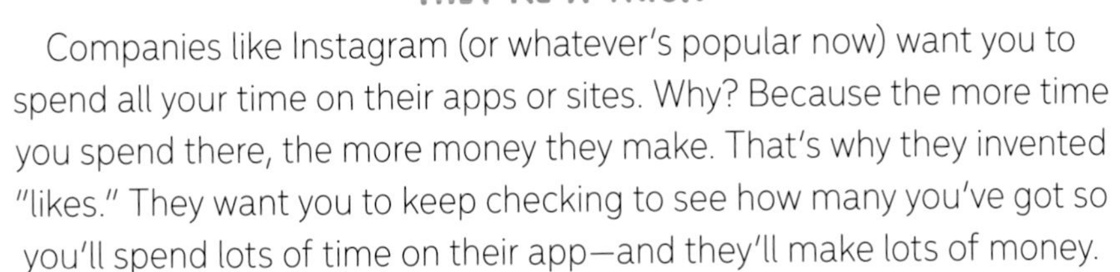

Companies like Instagram (or whatever's popular now) want you to spend all your time on their apps or sites. Why? Because the more time you spend there, the more money they make. That's why they invented "likes." They want you to keep checking to see how many you've got so you'll spend lots of time on their app—and they'll make lots of money.

THEY WASTE YOUR TiME

Some people spend hours and hours checking to see how many likes they've got. You know what they could be doing with all that time? HAVING FUN. Turn off the computer. Put the phone down. Then go outside and do something.

THEY CAN MAKE PEOPLE FEEL BAD FOR NO REASON

Believe it or not, there are people out there who get really sad when something they post doesn't get a bunch of likes. This is ridiculous. Who cares what other people think? Just be you! If you spend all of your time trying to please other people, you'll never discover the things that make YOU happy.

LiKES DON'T MEAN ANYTHING

When you're 100 years old, nobody's going to care if a picture of your new outfit got 10,000 likes. Heck, nobody's going to give a darn when you're 12! You know what will matter? The places you discovered, the things you invented, the bugs you ate, and all the amazing stories you have to tell. So if you really want to impress everyone, get off your butt and get started!

BE A SECRET SUPERHERO

You might be the sort of person who doesn't love attention. I get it! I'm a bit like that, too. But being shy doesn't mean you can't do good deeds. In fact, being awesome in secret can be even more fun. Here are a few secret superheroes you could be:

THE INVISIBLE FRIEND

Wait until no one's watching—and then leap into action! Find something that needs to be fixed, cleaned, or organized. Did the handle break off of your mom's favorite mug? Glue it back on. Is the refrigerator a disgusting disaster? Hold your nose and tidy it up. Does your dad's car need a good wash? Then hose it down while he's mowing the back lawn! When you've finished, return to whatever you were doing, act totally natural, and wait for the good deed to be discovered. Feel free to blame ghosts, elves, or brownies.

FLOWER KID

I believe flowers have magical powers. Yes, I'm totally serious! There's nothing more enchanting than finding a lovely flower growing in an unexpected place. So when spring comes, get a small packet of seeds. As you walk around, plant them in spots that could use something beautiful. When the flowers pop up, tell little kids it's a sign that fairies are around.

THE PEN PAL

This is the easiest way to make someone's whole day. (Maybe even their week!) Get a small scrap of paper and write down a compliment. Keep it sweet and simple. "Your sweater is AMAZING." Or "I'm really impressed that you ate those crickets." Or "Your history presentation was awesomely disgusting." Don't sign the note. Just slip it into your friend's backpack or book.

THE GIFT GIVER

Why stop with a note? Leave a little something for friends or family to find. You don't even need to spend money. Slip them a piece of gum at just the right moment. (If you're feeling SUPER generous, leave a whole pack!) Or how about leaving them one of those beautiful flowers you planted? Nothing makes people feel better like flowers and candy. PS: I really love Fireballs. Just saying.

THE PHILANTHROPIST

Do you have toys you no longer play with? Books you've read 10,000 times? Clothes you've outgrown? I bet you do. Why not share them with someone who could use them? Ask an adult to help you find a place to donate your things. Make sure they're clean and in good shape. Then pack them up nicely and deliver them to the charity of your choice!

11 THINGS TO DO BEFORE YOU TURN 11

1. LEARN HOW TO START A FIRE (SAFELY!) WITHOUT MATCHES.
2. FIND THREE COOL SPOTS IN YOUR NEIGHBORHOOD THAT YOU NEVER KNEW WERE THERE.
3. CREATE A MAP OF YOUR NEIGHBORHOOD WITH ALL THE BEST SPOTS.
4. LEARN HOW TO USE A FISHING POLE AND CATCH A FISH.
5. MAKE A BACKYARD SALAD. (OR A PARK SALAD IF YOU'RE A CITY KID.)
6. FIND ONE WAY YOU CAN MAKE THE WORLD A BETTER PLACE—AND DO IT.
7. EAT SOME BUGS OR STAGE A BEETLE BATTLE.
8. KEEP A CALENDAR AND WAKE YOURSELF UP FOR SCHOOL.
9. START TAKING CARE OF YOUR PETS. (THAT MEANS FEEDING AND POOP REMOVAL.)
10. MAKE MONEY OF YOUR OWN AND SAVE UP FOR SOMETHING YOU REALLY WANT.
11. TEACH SOMEONE WHO'S JUST TURNED 10 HOW TO DO SOME OF THE THINGS YOU LEARNED THIS YEAR.

ACKNOWLEDGMENTS

This series began as a birthday present for my daughter, Georgia, and her best friend, Wyatt. I owe Wyatt and his mom, Stephanie Kim Simons, my eternal gratitude for their friendship, enthusiasm, and encouragement.

Thanks as always to Suzanne Gluck and Andrea Blatt at WME for their tireless support. Andrea deserves a medal—or maybe a statue built in her honor. For now, I hope this acknowledgment will suffice!

This series would not have been possible without Anne Heltzel at Abrams, who shared my vision from the very beginning, and Hana Nakamura, who brought that vision to life.

And thanks to Michael Buckley, the funniest man on earth and one of the few adults who know how to enjoy life like a 10-year-old.

ABOUT THE AUTHOR

KIRSTEN MILLER is a renowned author of middle-grade and YA fiction. She lives in Brooklyn with her precocious 10-year-old, who helped write this book. Find out more at kirstenmillerbooks.com.

DON'T MISS

FOR ALL THE BEST SECRETS
ABOUT TURNING 8 AND 9!